Historic Churches of
Fredericksburg

MICHAEL AUBRECHT

HISTORIC CHURCHES OF
FREDERICKSBURG

HOUSES OF THE HOLY

Charleston · London

THE
History
PRESS

Published by The History Press
Charleston, SC 29403
www.historypress.net

Copyright © 2008 by Michael Aubrecht
All rights reserved

Cover image: From the original painting by Mort Künstler, *Changing of the Pickets*. ©2001 Mort Künstler, Inc.
www.mkunstler.com.

First published 2008

Manufactured in the United States

ISBN 978.1.59629.393.9

Library of Congress Cataloging-in-Publication Data

Aubrecht, Michael.
Historic churches of Fredericksburg : houses of the holy / Michael Aubrecht.
p. cm.
Includes bibliographical references.
ISBN 978-1-59629-393-9
1. Fredericksburg (Va.)--Church history. 2. Churches--Virginia--Fredericksburg. I. Title.
BR560.F8A93 2008
277.55'36609034--dc22
2008025714

This book is dedicated to my lovely wife, Tracy, and my children, Dylan, Madison, Kierstyn and Jackson, who are blessings in my life and the source of my happiness.

CONTENTS

ACKNOWLEDGEMENTS

Many Southern-based historians who specialize in the history of the Confederacy, myself included, tend to approach this period as if we are in a "bubble" of sorts. As a result, we often find ourselves writing strictly from the perspectives of the white Southern Secessionists. And although I vehemently maintain that it is extremely important to honor and acknowledge this aspect of our heritage, we also have to recognize that there were two other groups of citizens who were sharing the same wartime experience. These would be the local Unionists and the African American population. Therefore, there are actually three different perspectives to consider when reviewing Fredericksburg, Virginia's history during the War Between the States. With this book, I hope to encompass all of them, in order to present a more complete narrative with regard to the town's landmark churches.

I would like to add that it is not my intent to paint a negative impression of any of these fine churches and, as such, I have tried to maintain a balance. This includes multiple perspectives of the events surrounding the political, social and spiritual issues that challenged the antebellum South in the nineteenth century. The sensitive nature of secession, states' rights and the institution of slavery, as well as other racial tensions and injustices, have been acknowledged here when applicable. Some of the verbiage that is used in this book, specifically when quoting slaves and/or overseer narratives, may contain racial slurs. These have been kept in their entirety for historical accuracy and to illustrate period-speak. In some cases conflicting recollections are presented while giving equal weight to both sides of the story. I have also labored to present both the Federal and Confederate soldiers' points of view. It is my hope that by sharing these accounts, however uncomfortable they may be at times, I can pay tribute to the congregations of today whose ancestors survived the "Great Divide" to form a much stronger community.

I would also like to thank the following individuals for their generous help and support with regard to this project. Without them, this endeavor would not have come to fruition. God bless you all.

Thank you Gwen Woolf, my mentor and editor from the *Free Lance-Star*, who originally suggested me to The History Press as a potential author. Thank you THP staff, including Daniel Gidick, Lee Handford, Julie Foster, Laura All and Hilary McCullough, for seeing my manuscript through to press. Thank you Benjamin Smith, my managing editor at *Civil War Historian* magazine, for publicly supporting and promoting this project right from the start. Thank you, Fredericksburg/Spotsylvania National Military Park historians (especially John Hennessy, who provided both content consultation and photo research assistance) and Eric Mink, as well as the staff at Chatham Manor, who generously granted me access to their archives and tolerated my many inquiries with graceful patience. Thank you fellow Civil War authors Richard G. Williams Jr., Eric Wittenberg and the rest of the gang listed on Civil War Interactive for your expertise and advice. Also, to the wonderful folks at the Civil War Home Chatroom, I say thanks for plugging me into your world and staying interested in this project. Thank you Al Stone and the rest of the gentlemen from Lee's Lieutenants for welcoming me into your camp and giving me a venue to present and promote this work. Thank you Mr. Mort Kunstler for calling me "friend" and inspiring me to be the best that I can be. To my associates, Colleen Quinnell and Tarver Harris, I say thanks for the encouragement and the freedom to pursue this project. To my pastors, Reverend Alan Hager and Reverend Mike Motsko, whose spiritual guidance motivates me in all that I do, I say thank you for the many prayers and blessings. To my mother, Linda Aubrecht, I say thank you for always supporting this book and everything else that I do (even if I did move south and "join" the Confederacy). To my sister, Melissa Parks, I say thank you for not becoming a writer too, and stealing the limelight. To my father, Thomas Aubrecht, I say thank you for the edits, the trips and the weekend at Gettysburg in 1978 that started it all. To my children, I say thanks for the quiet time so daddy could type. And to my beautiful wife Tracy, who has been at my side since we were just teenagers and is literally nine months pregnant as I type this, thank you for EVERYTHING (and much much more).

I would also like to express my sincere gratitude to the following individuals who represented each of the churches that are featured in this book. Their dedication to the preservation and presentation of each congregation's history, along with their grace and generosity in sharing it, enabled me to gather a plethora of primary source information. Thank you for your hospitality:

Fredericksburg Baptist Church: Dennis Sacrey, church administrator
Shiloh Baptist (Old Site): Mark Olsen, Archives Committee
St. George's Episcopal Church: Trip Wiggins, church historian
Fredericksburg Presbyterian Church: Dori DeMild, communication assistant, and Sam Burgess, former member
Fredericksburg United Methodist Church: Becky Guy, church historian
University of Mary Washington: Dawn S. Bowen, PhD, photographer

Introduction

BATTLEFIELDS AND
BELIEVERS

The recent war…has so impoverished our people, and crippled our resources that I have refrained from urging upon your attention such measures…because of the inability of the people to meet the expenditures involved in their execution.

—*Fredericksburg mayor, 1866*

In order to understand the experiences of the historic churches of Fredericksburg, one must first look at the locality and the important role that organized religion played in the town. Today, the town is known as "America's Most Historic City," while the neighboring county of Spotsylvania is referred to as the "Crossroads of the Civil War." Both are literally saturated with landmark homesteads, museums, plantations and battlefields that draw thousands of tourists each and every year. Churches remain among some of the most coveted attractions for their historical significance and architectural beauty.

Fredericksburg has also been referred to as a "city of churches," as its silhouette is dominated by a plethora of bell towers and steepled roofs. Today there are over three hundred congregations spread throughout the surrounding region. Clearly, anyone walking through the town can see the important role religion played in the day-to-day lives of the town's inhabitants. Chartered in 1728, the settlement served as the surrounding area's political, social and economic center. As it was conveniently located on the banks of the Rappahannock River, Fredericksburg quickly became a bustling metropolis, with taverns, lodging and commerce. Both eighteenth- and nineteenth-century industries such as mills, shipping and transportation helped to establish the town as a commercial beacon on the ever-expanding map of central Virginia.

Despite a widespread disenchantment among America's first settlers with the Church of England, religion remained a precious keystone in colonial life. Many of the area's first citizens still retained their belief in God and brought the deep desire to practice their faith with them when they came to this new land. It was the freedom to pursue that faith in a variety of forms that separated the early Protestant and even Catholic churches from their European counterparts. Therefore, churches were significantly important institutions in the foundation of any settlement in the New World.

Fredericksburg Courthouse today. *Courtesy Fredericksburg Tourism.*

The original English settlement of Fredericksburg had been clustered in a fifty-acre area along the west bank of the river. It was originally engineered in a grid-like pattern, with wide streets that were named after British royalty. The initial plot consisted of sixty-four equally sized lots with two extra spaces for a church and a market. As the population increased, Fredericksburg found it necessary to expand the municipal boundaries. By 1759, the city had tripled its physical size, opening the door to both new merchants and settlers alike. Eventually, the boundary line was pushed westward toward the area known as the "Sunken Road." This hallowed ground witnessed the brunt of the Battle of Fredericksburg and is a national military park today.

Historically, the town of Fredericksburg is especially noteworthy with regard to all American faiths. It was here, at an establishment known as Weedon's Tavern, where Thomas Jefferson met with his political contemporaries in 1777 and agreed to author a bill for religious liberties in America. Today, the Religious Freedom Monument stands as a testament to that event. The simple marker was first unveiled in 1932 and consists of a small obelisk made of hewn stone blocks. It is a tribute to Jefferson's words, which resulted in the Virginia Statute of Religious Freedom.

The statute, enacted in 1786, separated church and state and gave equal status to all faiths. It became the basis for the First Amendment to the U.S. Constitution, giving all Americans the freedom to practice the religion of their choice or none at all. Jefferson himself proclaimed this bill to be one of his three proudest achievements, alongside authoring the Declaration of Independence and founding the University of Virginia. In fact, these three accomplishments are the only ones that he deemed worthy to inscribe on his grave marker at Monticello.

In 1828, Fredericksburg residents realized that the development of their city was seriously lagging behind the nearby cities of Alexandria (to the north) and Richmond (to the south). As a result, they launched a thirty-year improvement plan that included a water navigation system and road improvements. Fredericksburg also wanted to compete with the nearby town of Falmouth, which had established a stable economy based on the industrial processing of flour. By 1830, both towns collectively boasted a flour-inspection rate of 125,000 barrels a year. However, output dropped dramatically to under 60,000 barrels annually in 1847. This decline hurt the local economy and did nothing to help cover the costs of the city's fledging revitalization plans.

Unfortunately, many of Fredericksburg's long-term projects proved to be poorly planned or executed. By 1858, most had fallen into bankruptcy after uncoordinated and intermittent attempts to complete them were unsuccessful. The news editors of the *Semi-Weekly News*, *Christian Banner* and *Weekly Advertiser* spared no words when they wrote pieces taking the citizens to task for their "lack of energy and enterprise," as well as their penchant for mediocrity. Clearly the town's officials did not anticipate the requirements of their plans, nor did they prepare any contingencies in the event of failures.

Eventually many of these developmental matters were tended to, but a rift remained between the citizens of the city who found differences in social, political and spiritual aspects of life. Slaveholding was a particularly sensitive issue, as the town's white citizens were divided along pro- and antislavery lines. Numbers of influential white citizens held meetings at the town hall calling for the support of African colonization. These meetings were deemed unpopular by many, as the institution of slavery in the Old Dominion had been in place for generations.

Traced back to the earliest colonization of America, human bondage remained one of the most controversial aspects of the country's culture. The first Africans arrived in the New World as indentured servants at the Virginia Company's Jamestown Settlement in 1619. There, they were initially able to earn their freedom by working as laborers, artisans, servants and cooks for white European settlers. However, the role of indentured servant was radically redefined by 1640, when the colony of Maryland became the first settlement to officially institutionalize slavery. The practice was then propagated in the North in 1641, when Massachusetts legalized it by establishing in the legislative Body of Liberties that "bondage," in certain circumstances, was lawful. This act inevitably ushered in the ability for one human being to hold property ownership of another human being.

The early Christian churches did not take up the cause of eliminating slavery until much later in the century, and some church leaders attempted to justify the act by quoting passages from the Bible that outlined the proper treatment of slaves, specifically Deuteronomy 15:12–15, Ephesians 6:9 and Colossians 4:1. In 1693, the famous Boston theologian Cotton Mather wrote a propaganda piece titled "Rules for the Society of the Negroes," in which he argued that slavery had been spiritually sanctioned and that "Negroes were enslaved because they had sinned against God."

Town of Fredericksburg from across the river. *Courtesy U.S. National Park Service.*

Princess Anne Street, circa 1860s. *Courtesy U.S. National Park Service.*

Fredericksburg Courthouse, circa 1860s. *Courtesy U.S. National Park Service.*

Office of U.S. Sanitary Commission. *Courtesy U.S. National Park Service.*

Above: Fredericksburg from Marye's Heights. *Courtesy U.S. National Park Service.*

Left: Confederate General Robert E. Lee. *Courtesy Library of Congress.*

Right: Union General Ambrose E. Burnside.
Courtesy Library of Congress.

Below: Federal wounded at Fredericksburg.
Courtesy Library of Congress.

Union artillery on Stafford Heights. *Courtesy Library of Congress.*

Union pontoon crossing the river. *Courtesy U.S. National Park Service.*

Fredericksburg mill and bridge damage. *Courtesy Library of Congress.*

Fredericksburg house damage. *Courtesy Library of Congress.*

Fredericksburg streets in ruins. *Courtesy Library of Congress.*

The dead behind stone wall at sunken road. *Courtesy Library of Congress.*

Wounded soldiers at Fredericksburg. *Courtesy Library of Congress.*

Virginia contraband family. *Courtesy Library of Congress.*

Left: U.S. Sanitary
Commission depot.
Courtesy Library of Congress.

Below: Members of U.S.
Sanitary Commission.
Courtesy Library of Congress.

By 1833, a movement was underway to end the institution of slavery, as organizations such as the American Anti-Slavery Society—which later boasted such prominent black members as Frederick Douglass, Sojourner Truth and Harriet Tubman—came to fruition. Many white abolitionists, mostly Northerners, joined the movement that used a mix of social and political methods to bring attention to the suffering of the slave population. With an economy that was heavily dependent on forced labor, the Southern states, including Virginia, were less than eager to emancipate the slaves. This led to a strong divide between the citizens on both sides of the issue.

Renowned British author Charles Dickens recalled a trip to Fredericksburg, where he boarded a train with a detestable passenger who was a "champion of Life, Liberty, and the Pursuit of Happiness" and had just "separated a slave family through his purchase." A European visitor to the town wrote to his relatives that he had been awakened by the cries of a Negro who was undergoing a "severe correction."

In 1842, the Englishman James Buckingham published his own description of an encounter with a group of owned Africans while passing through the area toward Falmouth. He wrote:

> In a valley near this [town], we met a gang of slaves, including men, women, and children, the men chained together in pairs, and the women carrying the children and bundles, in their march to the South. The gang was under several white drivers who rode near them on horseback, with large whips…and there was one driver behind…They were chained together for precaution rather than for punishment.

Of all the accounts regarding suffrage in the Fredericksburg/Spotsylvania area, perhaps none is as disturbing as those from the field hands themselves. Regardless of the popular notion of a pastoral antebellum South filled with the romance and pageantry of *Gone with the Wind*, the day-to-day lives of those held in bondage were filled with fear and misery. One Spotsylvania slave reminisced on an experience he had suffered during a wheat harvest in 1855. He recalled:

> I was cradling—I couldn't make the cradle cut well. S—[the owner] said, "You can make that cradle cut better if you choose to…but you don't choose to." I told him I had tried to make it do the best I know how. Then he said to the men, "Come here and take hold of this d—d nigger, I'll make it all right with him." Then he took me to the barn…While he was tying me up, I told him, I will do all I know how to do. He said "[I]t was a d—d lie"…but he knew I could do it…and when he was done with me, he'd show that I would do it. Then he commenced to whipping me…Before he took me down, he said, "Now will you go and do the business?" I told him then, that "I had told [you] before that I would willingly do all I knew how."

In 1858, almost half of the 150-member congregation at the Fredericksburg United Methodist Church was publicly chastised by its fellow believers for "harboring a deep rooted hostility toward the institution of slavery." There were many Methodists who were willing to stand up against the practice, no matter how unpopular their views were among the denomination's proslavery parishioners.

This wasn't the first time such a debate raged. In 1844, the Methodist church had already split over the issue of slavery, forming two congregations. Methodist Church (North) was located on the site of the current church and Methodist Church (South) was located on George Street. For about a decade, there was also a separate black Methodist church in town, but it burned down in 1854. The neighboring Baptist church also featured an integrated congregation, with separate entrances and galleries for slaves and free blacks, until 1855. Then the white members moved to the new sanctuary and sold the old church to the black members for $500. Thus was born the African Baptist Church.

These newly formed institutions enabled the black congregations to worship together, although they still remained under the supervision of a white elder, who was required by law to supervise the proceedings. This paternalistic approach no doubt sullied the sincerity of goodwill that was directed toward the black worshipers. There were rare examples of white citizens compromising on the institution, but their efforts fell far short of true emancipation. One such example recalls the story of a local slave shoemaker named Noah Davis, who was assisted by Fredericksburg's prominent citizens as he pursued his family's freedom and a career as a minister. The Patton family, in particular, pledged to sell Davis his independence and allowed him to travel to raise the required funds. Neighboring families also helped. The Stevenson family agreed to sell his wife's freedom and the Wright family helped Davis to finance the purchase of his children.

Ms. Hannah Coalter of the palatial Chatham Manor offered all ninety-two of her slaves a choice between immigration and continued bondage after her death. Although the offer appears to be a generous one, it should be noted that it was on an individual basis and had no stipulation for keeping relatives together. This resulted in an agonizing choice of freedom over one's family. Coalter's successor, Horace Lacy, was not interested in granting freedom to any of Chatham's slaves. He filed a grievance with the Virginia Supreme Court system to overturn Ms. Coalter's offer. The court sided with the plaintiff, citing that the servant population of Fredericksburg was not considered citizenry and therefore had no right to make decisions regarding their release.

This powder-keg relationship between the town's different races provided an explosive backdrop for political discord. In 1860, many of the city's white citizens labored to prevent secession. Despite a very public and popular outrage over the John Brown revolt at Harpers Ferry, most residents continued to argue over the long-term benefits of such a drastic endeavor as dissolving the Union. The local newspapers fueled the fire of discontent with their angry remarks following the victory of Republican presidential candidate Abraham Lincoln. Most recommended economic boycotts and other nonviolent forms of protest.

As tempers continued to flare, the Fredericksburg Young Men's Christian Association initiated prayer meetings in both the local Baptist church and St. George's to seek divine intervention against the impending "anarchy that now prevails." The existing churches were often used during these times for both public discussions and petitions.

Union burial detail at Fredericksburg. *Courtesy U.S. National Park Service.*

Federal gravediggers preparing bodies. *Courtesy U.S. National Park Service.*

In the Senate of the United States,

February 28, 1905.

Resolved, That the claims of the trustees of the Fredericksburg Baptist Church, of Fredericksburg, Virginia (S. 5774); the
trustees of Zion Methodist Episcopal Church South, of Spottsylvania
County, Virginia (S. 5775); the Trustees of Saint George's Epis-
copal Church, of Fredericksburg, Virginia (S. 5776); the trustees
of the Methodist Episcopal Church, of Newtown, Virginia
(S. 5915); the trustees of the Methodist Episcopal Church at
Garys, Prince George County, Virginia (S. 5916); the trustees of
Market Street Methodist Episcopal Church, of Winchester, Vir-
ginia (S. 5917); the trustees of Saint Mary's Catholic Church, of
Fredericksburg, Virginia (S. 5918); the trustees of Warrenton
Academy, of Warrenton, Virginia (S. 5919); the trustees of the
Methodist Episcopal Church South, of Kernstown, Virginia (S.
5920); the trustees of Carters Run Baptist Church, of Fauquier
County, Virginia (S. 5921); the vestry of Zion Protestant Episco-
pal Church, of Fairfax, Virginia (S. 5922); the trustees of Ebe-
nezer Methodist Episcopal Church South, of Garrisonville, Virginia
(S.5923); the trustees of Grove Baptist Church, of Fauquier County,
Virginia (S.5924); the trustees of Shiloh (old site) Baptist Church,
of Fredericksburg, Virginia (S. 5925); the trustees of John Mann

U.S. Congress Claim Certificate, page 1. *Courtesy U.S. National Park Service.*

All the prayer and temperance meetings in the world, however, could not stop the call to arms.

A formal "Call for Secession" was sent out to all Southern states that did not agree with the proposed principles of newly elected President Lincoln. It was the dawning of some of the darkest years in American history, as brother turned against brother in the name of their cause. In 1861, the nearby city of Richmond was declared the capital of the newly christened Confederate States of America, following Jefferson Davis's inauguration as its president. In a letter sent to the Lincoln administration, Virginia vehemently declared its independence.

In retaliation, Lincoln issued his first executive order while calling for seventy-five thousand volunteers to suppress the Southern rebellion. America's Civil War had begun. What was initially expected to be a three-month affair would result in a four-year conflict that cost millions of dollars in damage and killed 2 percent of the country's population.

Four major battles took place on Fredericksburg and Spotsylvania soil over the next four years, scarring the countryside and forever securing the area's significance in

2

Methodist Episcopal Church (colored), of Winchester, Virginia (S. 5926); Fairfax Lodge, Numbered Forty-three, Ancient Free and Accepted Masons, of Culpeper, Virginia (S. 5927); the trustees of Saint Paul's Free Church, of Fauquier County, Virginia (S. 5928); the trustees of Saint Paul's Lutheran Church, of Stephens City, Virginia (S. 5929); the trustees of the Wilderness Baptist Church, of Spottsylvania County, Virginia (S. 6173); the trustees of Liberty Church, Dranesville, Virginia (S. 6397); the trustees of the Presbyterian Church, of Marshall, Virginia (S. 6398); the vestry of Saint James Protestant Episcopal Church, of Culpeper County, Virginia (S. 6399); the trustees of Mount Zion Old School Baptist Church, near Aldie, Loudoun County, Virginia (S. 6400); the trustees of the Methodist Episcopal Church South, of Jeffersonton, Culpeper County, Virginia (S. 6401); the trustees of High Hill Baptist Church, of Greenesville County, Virginia (S. 6569); the trustees of the Presbyterian Church of Fredericksburg, Virginia (S. 6797); the trustees of the Methodist Episcopal Church South, of Warrenton, Virginia (S. 6845); the trustees of New Hope Baptist Church, of Orange County, Virginia (S. 6959); the Alfred Street Baptist Church (colored), of Alexandria, Virginia (S. 7053); the vestry of the Episcopal Church of The Plains, Fauquier County, Virginia (S. 7067); the trustees of the Methodist Episcopal Church South, of Suffolk, Nansemond County, Virginia (S. 7068); the vestry of Saint Paul's Protestant Episcopal Church, of Haymarket, Prince William County, Virginia (S. 7243); and the trustees of Lebanon

3

Union Church, of Lincolnia, Fairfax County, Virginia (S. 7245), now pending in the Senate, together with all the accompanying papers, be, and the same are hereby, referred to the Court of Claims, in pursuance of the provisions of an Act entitled "An Act to provide for the bringing of suits against the Government of the United States," approved March third, eighteen hundred and eighty-seven, and generally known as the Tucker Act. And the said court shall proceed with the same in accordance with the provisions of such Act, and report to the Senate in accordance therewith.

Attest:

Charles L. Bennett

Secretary.

Left: U.S. Congress Claim Certificate, page 2.
Courtesy U.S. National Park Service.

Above: U.S. Congress Claim Certificate, page 3.
Courtesy U.S. National Park Service.

America's history books. Today, each site is a protected battlefield that is maintained by the National Park Service. This includes Fredericksburg (December 11 through December 15, 1862), Chancellorsville (April 30 through May 6, 1863), the Wilderness (May 5 through May 7, 1864) and Spotsylvania Court House (May 8 through May 21, 1864).

These pivotal engagements touched the town of Fredericksburg in different ways. The most prominent was the battle that took place within and immediately around the community boundaries. In December of 1862, Federal troops from the Army of the Potomac, commanded by Major General Ambrose E. Burnside, crossed over the Rappahannock River on pontoon bridges and entered the city of Fredericksburg. What followed was one of the most one-sided Confederate victories of the entire Civil War.

The Union's occupation followed a massive bombardment that left much of the town's structures in shambles. It was the first recorded incident of the shelling of a town in America and although the results were severe, the action itself was justified from a military standpoint. Despite evacuating much of the civilian population, the Confederates had left behind a contingent of sharpshooters and skirmishers to wreak

Fredericksburg National Cemetery. *Courtesy U.S. National Park Service.*

Fredericksburg "refugees" painting. *Courtesy D.E. Henderson/Gettysburg Museum.*

Battered homes along Hanover Street. *Courtesy National Archives.*

Confederates at the Sunken Road. *Courtesy Museum of the Confederacy.*

Pontoon crossing (note the churches in the background). *Courtesy U.S. National Park Service.*

Federal troops looting Fredericksburg. *Courtesy National Archives/NMP.*

havoc on the engineering corps that was working to assemble the floating bridges. Their presence warranted the use of artillery on the city.

Once in possession of the battered town, the Federals faced a near impossible task of moving forward, as Major General Robert E. Lee had positioned the artillery and infantry of his Army of Northern Virginia on the heights above the city, as well as in entrenched positions below. This brilliant tactical strategy dealt a devastating blow to the Union army, which was forced to conduct a series of doomed assaults while attempting to march across an open field toward an impenetrable stone wall at the base of Marye's Heights.

The *Richmond Examiner* described the encounter as a "stunning defeat to the invader, a splendid victory to the defender of the sacred soil." General Lee, normally reserved, was described in the *Charleston Mercury* as "jubilant, almost off-balance, and seemingly desirous of embracing everyone who calls on him." The newspaper also exclaimed, "General Lee knows his business and the army has yet known no such word as fail."

The carnage that resulted from these engagements was staggering. In an article published in the *London Times* on January 23, 1863, a reporter penned a portrait of death and destruction:

> *It remains for me to give some account of the town of Fredericksburg, and the condition in which it was left by its ruthless invaders. Desolate it had appeared to me at the end of last month; how shall I describe its appearance now? The first impression of those who rode into its streets, and who had witnessed the deu d'enfer which the Federal guns had poured upon it for hours upon Thursday, the 11th of December, was surprise that more damage had not been done. But this is explained by the fact that the Federals confined themselves almost entirely to solid round shot, and that very few shells were discharged into the town. Nevertheless a more pitiable devastation and destruction of property would be difficult to conceive. Whole blocks of buildings have in many places been given to the flames. There is hardly a house through which at least one round-shot has not bored its way, and many are riddled through and through. The Baptist church is rent by a dozen great holes, while its neighbour, The Episcopalian Church, has escaped with one. Scarcely a spot can be found on the face of the houses which look toward the river which is not pockmarked by bullets. Everywhere the houses have been plundered from cellar to garret; all smaller articles of furniture carried off, all larger ones wantonly smashed. Not a drawer or chest but was forced open and ransacked. The streets were sprinkled with the remains of costly furniture dragged out of the houses in the direction of the pontoons stretched across the river. Many of the inhabitants clung to the town, and sheltered themselves during the shelling in cellars and basements. Among others, it is stated that Mrs. Slaughter, the wife of the Mayor, returned two or three days after the bombardment to her house, which she found ransacked and gutted. A Federal officer offered a few words of explanation or apology, when she replied, pointing to half a dozen dead Federals lying within site of her house, "I am repaid for all I have suffered by the sight of these."*

Despite the overwhelming Confederate victory at the Battle of Fredericksburg, the damage to the city's infrastructure could not have come at a worse time, as the city was finally beginning to reap some economic prosperity. In an 1860 issue, *DeBow's Review* reported that Fredericksburg was "still alive and growing," and that the city was "beautiful and healthful, her attractiveness growing out of the high character of her population." It added, "People now go there to live on their incomes, educate their families, and enjoy intellectual, moral, and religious social intercourse." This, however, was only speaking of the white population, as slaves were not able to enjoy any of these liberties.

Over the next few years, Americans battled from all points north, south, east and west. When the smoke cleared, over 600,000 soldiers had died and much of the South lay in ruins. Churches were also trying to recover from the residual damage to their sanctuaries, as well as the loss of so many young men from their flocks. Fredericksburg, in particular, had several of its churches severely damaged in the attack on the city in December of 1862. Most of the churches had been used as makeshift field hospitals and periodic headquarters throughout the war. Cannon shot, fire, blood and graffiti had damaged the exteriors and interiors of the structures. Like many of the soldiers who were treated within the walls of these sacred institutions, it would be years before the town and its surrounding countryside would recover from the wounds of war.

Today, Fredericksburg remains a favorite destination in central Virginia. Thousands of tourists from all over the world journey to the city to take in its history, art, antiques and culture. Historic markers, monuments and museums, as well as miles of Civil War trails, dominate the landscape of the area. Among the most treasured and frequently photographed landmarks of the city are its numerous houses of worship that dominate the upper streets and riverfront portions of Fredericksburg. The expansion of the town's piety out to the rural landscape of Spotsylvania County also presents visitors with a wonderful driving tour of historic country churches. Many of them grew out of the city's original congregations, either by chartered expansion or by divisions within the denominations.

Their chronicles are as similar as can be in some respects, yet as different as night and day in others. It is only through examining these multiple perspectives from local citizens of all colors and denominations who collectively witnessed their country's great divide that we can begin to understand the legacies of these historical churches. Each one of these buildings was filled with citizens and soldiers, black and white, who were forced to deal with great adversity in these troubled times.

FREDERICKSBURG BAPTIST CHURCH

A solid shot came crashing through the church walls, knocking the plastering in a furious shower over patients and surgeons. Lights were ordered out; all surgery ceased and the surgeons labored in the dark to render the wounded comfortable.
—*Union Surgeon William Child of the Fifth New Hampshire*

Background

Located at 1019 Princess Anne Street, the Fredericksburg Baptist Church was founded in 1804. It moved to its current location in 1855, following a split with the African members who remained at the original Sophia Street site, which is now Shiloh Baptist Church. The current Gothic Revival–style edifice was completed that same year. Fredericksburg Baptist Church remains the second-largest church building to stand within the city limits. During the War Between the States, the structure suffered extensive damage from Federal artillery fire prior to the city's occupation by Union forces during the Battle of Fredericksburg. Like many area churches, the pews were torn out and the sanctuary was used as a Federal field hospital. Today, the building remains much the way it did after the war damage was repaired.

Church Origin

According to records from the early 1800s, the first "official" Baptist Meeting House (a prelude to a sanctioned house of worship) was established in Fredericksburg around 1803. The original sanctuary and its attendees included whites, slaves and free "Negroes." Nonwhite members were required to use side-door entrances and separate seating areas, as the interior space of the sanctuary was racially delineated. This trend would continue in churches throughout the South for years to come.

By 1818, the congregation was eager to construct a much larger, more permanent brick building. This resulted in the acquisition of the site at Shiloh Baptist Church (Old Site), which had previously belonged to the Bank of Virginia. Following a devastating

Fredericksburg Baptist Church.
Courtesy Dawn S. Bowen, PhD.

fire in October of 1807, the property had remained unused. In April of 1820, the lot owners, Horace Marshall and his wife Elizabeth, sold the property to the trustees of the New Baptist Meeting House for $900. It is believed that the first brick church structure was erected on the lot in the late 1830s, or even perhaps the very early 1840s.

Beginning with a small congregation, Fredericksburg Baptist Church persevered through the years and grew significantly in member numbers. Within a decade of its inauguration, the church boasted over eight hundred attendees on its rolls. Surprisingly, almost three fourths of its membership was made up of slaves and free blacks. This multiracial fellowship represented what may be considered a hypocritical dichotomy, as Christians appeared able to come together on Sundays to celebrate the Sabbath, yet remained separatists during the rest of the week.

One of the city's most respected ministers resided at Fredericksburg Baptist and would later become one of Fredericksburg's first unwilling civilian participants in the Civil War. His name was Reverend William F. Broaddus, and he was called upon to assume the pastorship of the church in 1853. It was under his supervision and guiding hand that the construction of the new church came to fruition. This event, however, resulted in a

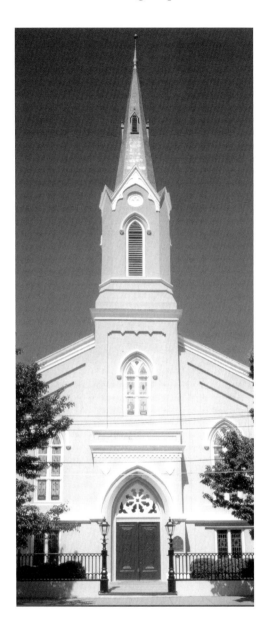

Fredericksburg Baptist tower today. *Courtesy Fredericksburg Baptist Church*.

controversial split between black and white members of the congregation. An amicable solution resulted in the birth of two independent churches. The memories surrounding this division vary depending upon which congregation is queried.

At the time the expansion was proposed, there were approximately 625 African American members in the Fredericksburg Baptist congregation. This group incorporated a large number of black slaves who had been granted permission by their masters to attend services on Sunday at the same time that they attended. In 1854, tensions began to develop between the two races, and their separation appeared to be a foregone conclusion.

Elder George Rowe portrait. *Courtesy U.S. National Park Service.*

A pledge drive was established to assist in financing the construction of a newer and larger building. Despite their limited resources and their social situation, the black members were able to raise an impressive sum of money. In the congregational minutes book that was dated September 28, 1855, the congregation's "colored brethren and sisters" pledged $1,100. It was then determined that the African American members would retain the current building by the riverside, and the white congregation would take all pledges and construct a new building in the center of town. A committee was appointed to oversee the matter. When the "colored brethren" expressed a strong opposition to the fulfillment of pledges for another church, a compromise of $400 ($500 according to Shiloh's accounts) was agreed upon.

A new constitution was drafted that dismissed the "colored congregation" and designated the existing church as a separate body named the African Baptist Church of Fredericksburg. A special provision was included, stating that in case of any difficulty in the transaction of business, the church may appeal to the Fredericksburg Baptist Church for counsel. It also went on to state, "The church pledges herself to listen to and regard the counsels of the committee of the white brethren that may be appointed by the Fredericksburg Baptist Church to superintend our worship according to the requirements of the law." (Under Virginia law, a white minister had to preside over a black congregation.)

In January of 1857, the *Fredericksburg Recorder* reported that the African church had added another one hundred members and "their assemblages are conducted

Right: Reverend William Broaddus. *Courtesy U.S. National Park Service.*

Below: Fredericksburg Baptist, circa 1860s. *Courtesy Library of Congress.*

in a remarkable quiet and orderly manner, and we are gratified to see them so fully appreciate their religious privileges."

The white congregation, consisting of more than 250 members, went off to construct its own house of worship. Despite suffering a public scandal over the adulterous lifestyle of a female member and several embarrassing financial faults, the Baptists managed to overcome great adversities and build one of the most prosperous churches in the region. The doors to the new Fredericksburg Baptist sanctuary opened to the public in 1855.

Soon after, the *Recorder* published another article praising the new church:

> *We must congratulate our Baptist friends that they posses a house of worship so elegant and well appointed. We should be ungrateful to pass by without compliment the excellent music discoursed by the Choir attached to this congregation. Its music is a great attraction and reflects credit upon those who, by their zeal and perseverance, have attained such perfection.*

Both churches were intimately touched by the War Between the States and remain in full operation at their original locations today.

The War

One of the most memorable highlights of Fredericksburg Baptist Church history, during the Civil War, took place months before any battle raged in its vicinity. This controversial event involved the seizure of several prominent civilians in the summer of 1862. Despite the initial impression, these retaliatory arrests were acceptable, as military protocol allowed the use of prisoners for exchanges early on in the war. As the conflict continued, the parole and subsequent release of POWs, especially members of the Confederate army, became prohibited as the popular belief was that the release of prisoners back onto the battlefield only prolonged the hostilities.

In July of 1862, a Union blockade of the surrounding area, and the intermittent occupation of the city by Federal forces, weighed heavily upon the lives of the citizens of Fredericksburg and Spotsylvania. As tensions increased, General Pope ordered a subordinate captain to arrest several civilians from the town in hopes that it would secure the release of captured Unionists who had been taken to Richmond and possibly force the community into a submissive mode. Several men who were considered to be influential in the community were targeted. Among them was Fredericksburg Baptist's own beloved preacher, the Reverend William F. Broaddus.

Archibald Thomas Robertson paid tribute to the abiding strength and wisdom of the minister in *Life and Letters of John Albert Broaddus* when he wrote:

> *Dr. Wm. F. Broaddus was a minister of great power. He left a deep impress on religious life in Virginia and Kentucky. Like most of the Baptist ministers of his time, he had limited opportunities for education, yet he added great industry to his unusual gifts. He*

was the warm friend of ministerial education and for some time acted as agent for the Southern Baptist Theological Seminary. He began preaching in Culpeper at the age of twenty in the early part of the century. He wrote an autobiography covering seven large manuscript volumes, but this was unfortunately burned with his house at Shelbyville, Ky. Once more he recorded his recollections, which were again destroyed in Fredericksburg when the town was captured by the Federal troops in 1862. In his closing years he again prepared brief reminiscences which have been preserved. Virginia Baptists and the whole South owe Dr. Wm. F. Broaddus a debt for his bold advocacy of the mission enterprise against the "Hardshell" or "Black Rock" element of the denomination, which was very strong in all Piedmont Virginia, the Valley and the Mountains.

According to the testimony of Lucy Ann Broaddus, an account of his forced incarceration stated:

On July 29, 1862, while walking along Main Street, Broaddus was arrested by the Federals and was taken to Old Capital Prison in Washington pending an exchange with Confederate prisoners. News traveled to the Broaddus home on that July day and Lucy and a slave, Hattie, came to bid farewell. In the words of Broaddus, the farewell was "a trial I would fain have escaped." For the next two months Lucy Ann sent packages of provisions to her husband. Eventually he was released and the welcoming was another tender scene.

It has been reported that the good reverend was a man who was widely known for his strong convictions, as well as his wonderful sense of humor. Several recollections of his time in prison paint the portrait of a man who was unwavering in his faith, regardless of his circumstances. It was also recorded that he had great fun at the expense of one of the Federal officers by insisting again and again that he, too, had no idea what the letter *F* in his name stood for. In actuality he had two *F*s in his name: Dr. William Francis Ferguson Broaddus. He also claimed not to know his native county. The Union officer was reportedly frustrated to the point of giving up the notion of getting any straight answers from the elusive missionary.

Broaddus was one of nineteen hostages abducted in direct retaliation for the arrest of local Unionist citizens who had been captured by the Confederate army. An educated man and talented wordsmith, the preacher kept an account of his experiences in prison through a daily diary, which was published years later under the title *The Prison Diary of William F. Broaddus.* His entries for his initial seizure stated:

Tuesday, July 29, 1862. While walking today near the Exchange at the corner of Main [Caroline] and Commerce street in Fredericksburg, I was stopped by Captain Scott of the Federal Army and informed that by the order of General King, I was under arrest to be taken at once to General King's headquarters. I asked the privilege of taking leave of my family, but this was declared to be unmilitary. I, however, met with Willie Slaughter on the street, and requested him to go to my residence for my trunk, to be brought to

General Patrick's headquarters at Farmer's Bank. Here I was kept about 30 minutes. During this half-hour my wife and Hattie came to take leave of me, a trial I would fain have escaped…

Arrived at the Lacy house, General King's headquarters. I was detained for more than an hour, and at 11:30 o'clock left on the cars for Aquia Creek, where I took the government boat for Washington. On the boat I met with Mr. and Mrs. William Gill and Mrs. Peyton Conway, on their way to Baltimore. This is fortunate for my comforts for besides giving me pleasure by their company; they permitted me to share their snack, which constituted the only refreshment I met with until I arrived at my prison. I found my fellow townsmen, C.C. Wellford, Thomas F. Knox, James McGuire, B.T. Gill and James H. Bradley, occupying one room. William Barton, who belonged to this mess, had been paroled and is in Baltimore. They had with them a Mr. Garnett of Spotsylvania County, a prisoner of war, who politely vacated his bunk and found a place in another room. By this means I secured the very great privilege of messing with my neighbors and friends.

Far from home, but still in the service of his Savior, Reverend Broaddus conducted Sunday services amidst the stockade of Federal prison. Among his comrades were several fellow members of the Fredericksburg Baptist Church. In August, Broaddus wrote as if the spirit of Saint Paul, who had also been imprisoned unjustly, filled him:

This is a beautiful morning! Oh how I long to be home. I find myself unconsciously conning a sermon. But I look around me and see nothing but dark walls and iron bars for my Sabbath temple. How long shall this cruel imprisonment last? Well perhaps I deserve it all for not having prized liberty as I ought to have done while I enjoyed it…We had a conference this morning as to the manner in which we shall spend the day. We are all called Christians, and feel disposed to honor the day that celebrates the resurrection of our Lord and Master. But we are surrounded with Federal deserters, guards, and detectives, and everything we say or do is closely watched.

One of the people whom Broaddus met while incarcerated was none other than the famous female Confederate spy, Ms. Belle Boyd. He remarked that she was "graceful" and that he could not help "admiring the spirit of patriotism, which seems to control her conduct, although much of romance is no doubt mixed with her patriotism."

Eventually, the preacher was granted a temporary parole pass to travel to the Confederate capital of Richmond in order to negotiate a prisoner exchange. Broaddus was successful in his mission, arranging for the release of twenty-five Unionists whose capture had initiated his entire ordeal. However, instead of immediately returning to the stronghold, the reverend took a detour to his hometown of Fredericksburg. He stopped at his beloved church to participate in a service and visit with members of his congregation until the early hours of the next morning. Then he surrendered himself to a Union soldier and requested to be taken back to the prison in Washington immediately. Instead of receiving the anticipated release for himself and his comrades, the pastor was sent back to his cell, where he waited for another two weeks before being set free.

During the second week of December 1862, the harsh reality of the Civil War came rolling over the city of Fredericksburg like a tidal wave. It all started with a shelling from 140 Union guns on the morning of December 11, two days before the actual battle had begun. It was the first recorded incidence of a city in the United States being bombarded by artillery fire and, reportedly, it was one of the loudest events ever to occur (to date) on American soil. The colossal barrage of cannon fire prior to Pickett's disastrous charge at Gettysburg would later top it. (Note: As all churches contained in this study witnessed the same battle, the first one will contain the summary of events from a military perspective. Those that follow will only contain their experiences as a result of the engagement.)

In a storm of "hellfire," whizzing shell fragments, tumbling bricks and raging fires engulfed the town. One Mississippian wrote, "Nothing in war can exceed the horror of that hour." The entire civilian population, black and white, was thrown into a panic. Some hid under tables in their basements, others ran into the countryside and several even attempted to swim to safety across the river. Following the cannonade, thousands of Union soldiers positioned themselves at the staging area at the base of Stafford Heights.

Despite the significant carnage levied on civilian structures, the Federal army had operated within a justified and predictable rule of engagement. Once Confederate Major General Robert E. Lee had decided to station sharpshooters as well as a small contingency of skirmishers in the town to harass the engineers who were attempting to assemble the pontoon bridges across the river, he had inevitably designated the city as a military threat. Lee's decision, however costly in damages, proved to be a logical choice.

By abandoning the town in favor of the heights beyond the city, Lee ultimately forced the Union army to come to him. In retrospect, the topographical advantages that were gained by the Army of Northern Virginia were essential to its victory. For the Army of the Potomac, the results of this tactic were catastrophic. It should also be noted that once the Union army occupied Fredericksburg, the Confederate artillery, too, turned itself on the town, which was now considered a military threat by virtue of the occupying forces.

After crossing the Rappahannock River on three sets of pontoon bridges and taking possession of the battered town, the Federal Army of the Potomac set its sights on taking the ridge where the Confederate Army of Northern Virginia had positioned itself. While awaiting orders to attack, many of the unsupervised soldiers took advantage of the officers' distractions and proceeded to loot homes and ransack businesses. Only after the arrival of senior commanders was order able to be established among the troops.

A Union soldier from the 132nd Pennsylvania recorded in his memoirs the looting of the town and subsequent rescue of a communion set by his chaplain. He wrote:

> *Many houses had fine pianos and other musical instruments, and in some instances impromptu dances were on whilst Confederate shells whanged through the house above their heads. It is safe to say that there was little left of valuable brica-brac to greet the*

fugitive people on their return. And it is highly probable that pianos and handsome furniture needed considerable repairing after the exodus of the "Yank." This was not due to pure vandalism, although war creates the latter, but to the feeling of hatred for the miserable rebels who had brought on the war and were the cause of us being there. And it must be admitted there were some who pocketed all they could for the commercialism there might be in it, the argument again being, "somebody will take it, and I might as well have it as the other fellow." The first part of the argument was doubtless as true as the latter part was false. Many trinkets were hawked about among the men after the fight as souvenirs. Among them was a silver-plated communion flagon. Some scamp had filched it from one of the churches and was trying to sell it. Fortunately, he did not belong to our regiment. Our chaplain took it from him and had it strapped to his saddle-bag. His purpose was to preserve it for its owner if the time should come that it could [be] returned. But in the meantime its presence attached to his saddle and made him the butt of any amount of raillery from both officers and men.

Prior to the arrival of the Federals, the vast majority of the town's white residents had evacuated their homes and fled into the hills. Many of the slaves who were left behind sought their own paths toward freedom and mingled among the Federal troops. Some of them later became stretcher bearers and wagon teamsters for the Union army. As the conflict continued, the contributions to the war effort by African Americans were advanced by the formation of "colored regiments" such as the Fifty-fourth Massachusetts.

By day's end, the infrastructure of Fredericksburg was in shambles. Homes were burned and businesses were reduced to rubble. Military preparation for the impending engagement was also underway, as Union troops commandeered many buildings and churches for use as headquarters and hospitals.

John B. Bailey of the Ninth New Hampshire Band participated in this process. He wrote about his duties for this matter in a diary entry dated December 13:

At an early hour Dr. Cutter called on fourteen men, seven from each Band, to go with him to the city, to establish hospitals there. Arrived there at daylight—and began at once to clear some residences of everything moveable, in a short time we had four ready for occupancy, we were then ordered to clear the Baptist Church, which was also done, while this was being done, the armies had met and the wounded were being rapidly brought in. In fact quicker than we had cleared them they were filled. Then in the outer rooms of the church the surgeons began to cut and slash, many limbs being no doubt needlessly lost. The battle continued throughout the day our troops gaining nothing, and at night—occupying the same ground as in the morning, during the day and night—the ambulances were carrying back the wounded, some without being attended to on the south side, and all who possibly could were ordered to walk.

These makeshift hospitals were in high demand, as General Lee had correctly anticipated the Federal army's plan and intentionally evacuated the town in order to

Baptist church damages. *Courtesy Library of Congress.*

1862

ported to Dr. Cutter, accompanied by members of the 2d Brig Band.
We were ordered to the rear of Stafford heights, and began to erect
hospital tents. Working at this all day, and remaining here through
the night. In the forenoon, our engineer corps not being able to lay
the pontoon bridges, on account of the enemies sharpshooters, being
secreted in the houses on the opposite banks. Gen Burnside ordered
the artillery on the heights to shell the city, after which the bridges
were laid and some of our forces crossed.

Dec 12th Our forces crossing all day on three bridges, and getting into position. We cutting pine and cedar twigs for beds for the wounded,
but few are brought in.

13th At an early hour Dr Cutter called for fourteen men, seven from
each Band, to go with him to the city, to establish hospitals there,
arrived there at daylight, and began at once to clear some residences
of everything moveable, in a short time we had four ready for occupancy. we were then ordered to clear the Baptist Church, which
was also done, while this was being done, the armies had met, and
the wounded were being rapidly brought in. In fact quicker than
we had cleared them they were filled. Then in the anterooms of the
Church the Surgeons began to cut and slash, many limbs being

A page from Union soldier John Baily's diary. *Courtesy U.S. National Park Service.*

fortify his army behind cover and on the high ground. As a highly educated and gifted tactician, Lee's strategy was as brilliant as it was simple: use the natural topography of the land as an advantage. The most impenetrable of the Rebels' positions was a long stone wall at the base of a sloping hill known as Marye's Heights. It soon became the site of a slaughter.

Wave after wave of bluecoats marched across the open field toward the stone wall to their deaths. It was, in retrospect, senseless killing, and an absolute disaster for the Union army commanding officer, General Ambrose Burnside, who had ignored repeated pleas from his subordinates to expedite and/or modify his battle plan. One of Lee's artillery officers, Colonel Edward Porter Alexander, had stated prior to the engagement that a "chicken couldn't live on that field." He was correct.

The death toll was staggering. In just one hour the Federals suffered more than three thousand dead. After fifteen unsuccessful charges, the fighting ceased, leaving the field littered with thousands of bloody Union bodies. Around midnight, Federal troops ventured forth under cover of darkness to gather what wounded they could find, but many were too close to the Confederate line to retrieve. Throughout the night, screams and cries of the wounded men penetrated the peaceful silence of the cease-fire.

One soldier, Richard Rowland Kirkland, an infantry sergeant with the Second South Carolina Volunteers, struggled to rest amidst the horrid sounds of suffering that echoed across the field. A combat veteran, he was accustomed to the dead and dying, having seen action at Manassas, Savage Station, Maryland Heights and Antietam. By the morning of December 14, he could take it no longer and requested permission to aid the enemy.

Initially, his commanding officer was reluctant, as Kirkland would likely be shot dead by Union sharpshooters when he cleared the wall. He later granted the persistent soldier his request, but forbid him to carry a flag of truce. With total disregard for safety, Kirkland grabbed several canteens and leaped over the fortification.

A fellow soldier in Kirkland's company later recalled the incident in part of a short narrative for the *Confederate Veteran* that was published in 1903. He wrote, "The enemy saw him and supposing his purpose was to rob the dead and wounded, rained shot and shell upon the brave Samaritan. God took care of him. Soon he lifted the head of one of the wounded enemy, placed the canteen to his lips and cooled his burning thirst. His motivation was then seen and the fire silenced. Shout after shout went up from friend and foe alike in honor of this brave deed."

In September of 1863, Kirkland was fighting in the western theatre with a detachment from Lieutenant General James Longstreet's corps, who had moved west to support Confederate General Braxton Bragg's efforts to stop the Army of the Cumberland. Longstreet's troops would do just that during the Battle of Chickamauga, which produced both a Southern victory and 34,600 casualties. Sadly, the then–Lieutenant Kirkland ranked among those killed during this colossal fight. Mortally wounded, Kirkland exhorted his comrades to "save yourselves," adding, "Tell Pa, I died right." Today Richard Kirkland is remembered as "the Angel of Marye's Heights."

Following the artillery bombardment of Fredericksburg, soldiers and war correspondents alike witnessed the destruction firsthand; much of it was inflicted on Fredericksburg's largest house of worship, the Baptist church on Princess Anne Street. Accounts printed in the *Richmond Enquirer* on December 13, 1862, stated:

> *The Baptist Church has been nearly riddled by shells, while all the pews have been torn out to make room for the sick, who were spread upon the pew cushions. The same condition of things was visible in the basement of the Episcopal Church. The Orphan Asylum, Dr. Scott's, F. Slaughter's, and S.S. Howison's houses were used as hospitals. In all, some twenty houses have been destroyed, and the loss of property of one kind or another cannot fall much short of $250,000.*

Thousands of wounded soldiers were moved back into the ruined city subsequent to the repeated charges. Virtually every public building was pressed into use as a hospital, as were some private residences. Churches provided the brunt of this service due to their large open sanctuaries, after being divested of the existing furniture. Despite being severely damaged by cannon shot, Fredericksburg Baptist Church became one of the largest "field" hospitals in the area.

In an article later published in the *American Journal of Medicine*, a Union surgeon recalled the church's contribution: "One of the principal hospitals was the Baptist Church, which was literally packed with wounded. The tank intended for immersion was used as a bathing tub, and the operations were performed in the pastor's small study, back of the pulpit."

Another surgeon, William Child of the Fifth Regiment, New Hampshire Volunteers, recalled the unforgettable stench of death and horrific sites that surrounded him. His experience was recorded in the following report:

> *Following a street [Amelia] up a hill...he saw dead men along the way, and at the top of the rising...saw shot from the enemy come bounding down the street...A farther advance in that direction not seeming discreet he turned to the left around the corner of a large church, used as a hospital, to whose director he reported for duty. Here he labored, dressing wounds until dark; the church floor being covered with Union wounded. Soon after dark candles were lighted, but after a brief quiet between sunset and dark, a solid shot came crashing through the church walls, knocking the plastering in a furious shower over patients and surgeons. Lights were ordered out; all surgery ceased and the surgeons labored in the dark to render the wounded comfortable.*

Despite having hundreds, perhaps even thousands of troops turned away over the course of two days, the Federal forces continued to attempt the desperate objective of seizing the stone wall and area at Marye's Heights. Throughout the course of the engagement, artillery fire from both sides continued to lob projectiles in and around the wounded city. Sometimes artillery shells would come crashing through the walls and roofs of buildings that had been designated as hospitals. These often resulted in horrific

View of Baptist steeple from Chatham. *Courtesy U.S. National Park Service.*

Fredericksburg Baptist (center). *Courtesy Thure de Thulstrup/Seventh Regiment Fund Inc.*

wounds being inflicted on those already hit and awaiting aid. It seemed, at times, as if no place in Fredericksburg was safe.

One soldier, Francis Edwin Pierce of the 108[th] New York Volunteer Infantry, found himself caught in the middle of one of these barrages. In a letter home he wrote:

> Co[mpanie]s A & F were standing between the church & Brick house [opposite the church on Princess Anne Street]. The [Confederate] battery at the head of the street['s axis on Marye's Heights] suddenly opened. The first shot just struck the corner of the house, knocked out a few bricks & exploded just as it struck the church. The 2nd shot passed entirely through the house & exploded just [as] it struck the church, 3rd shot[—]the same[,] only it exploded inside the church. Many of my company were seated on the curb stone in front of the church. The 4th shot passed entirely through the house but much lower than the others, so that it struck the curbstone…exploded & made awful work. Bob Collins…had his left leg taken off close to his body…It made a ghastly looking wound. Chas. Clark had his left arm knocked to pieces [and] also his left thigh & knee. Frank Downing was struck in the hip. John Sanders…[was] struck in about 4 or 5 places.

After the offensive ended, Union forces began withdrawing back across the pontoon bridges to the other side of the river. Many of their most seriously wounded who could not be moved were left behind to the care and compassion of the townsfolk, who were certainly relieved to see the enemy back on the other side of the Rappahannock. The Christian population was especially charitable, despite the deplorable conditions and nightmarish scenes that confronted them upon their return to the city. One letter published in the *Central Georgian* on December 18, 1862, described the tremendously bittersweet scene that greeted them:

> On Wednesday 17th I rode through the town and it was distressing to view the desolation. There is scarcely a house in the town that has not some mark of the siege, chimneys knocked off, roofs torn up, and walls scarred with holes of various sizes, some as large as a man's head and others as large as a barrel. The streets are covered with broken glass, window shutters and furniture of various descriptions. The large tall houses suffered more than the low buildings. A large Baptist Church has fifteen large holes through its walls, four through the steeple, and the roof torn up in many places. I think there are twenty-five or thirty houses burned. A few citizens remained in town secreted in cellars during the whole siege.

In her 1870 book *The Boys in White: The Experiences of a Hospital Agent In and Around Washington*, a nurse named Julia S. Wheelock recalled one soldier who managed to find light at Fredericksburg Baptist amidst the darkness of war:

> While distributing my crackers and soup to the inmates of a large church, where there are perhaps a hundred and fifty or two hundred poor sufferers lying side by side upon the floor, nearly all seriously and many mortally wounded, my ears were saluted with the voice of

song, and, looking around to see from whom it came, I saw a poor fellow with a severe wound in both arms, whom some one had raised up from his hard bed. He was sitting on the floor and leaning against the wall, singing as cheerfully, and apparently as joyously as if he were seated at the social hearth with his own dear family. It was a scene which brought tears to my eyes, for the voices of song strangely mixed with the dying groans, and I thought that one who could shut his eyes to the scenes of distress around him, and so far forget his sufferings as to attune his heart and voice to singing, must indeed have experienced the blessedness of the Christian's hope.

Reconstruction

Despite being a swift and decisive Confederate victory, the Federal army's presence at Fredericksburg left a long-standing impression on the town and its citizens, including members of the Baptist church. Even Reverend Broaddus relocated after closing the church as a result of the tremendous damage that was inflicted on its exterior and interior. The sanctuary had been left in shambles and the church's steeple was riddled with bullet holes and cannon shot.

No service was held at Fredericksburg Baptist Church from December of 1862 until the end of the war in 1865. Following the South's surrender at Appomattox, the residents of one of Virginia's oldest towns returned to begin the recovery and reconstruction process. With a strong resolve and determination, the Baptists managed to secure financial assistance from their Northern brethren. Little by little, the congregation began to pick up the pieces and repair the damage to its beloved sanctuary. Regular worship services soon followed, along with the appointment of a new pastor, the Reverend T.S. Dunaway, who would preach at their pulpit for the next thirty-two years.

Many of the churches that were involved in the Battle of Fredericksburg, or any battle for that matter, submitted itemized claims to the court of the United States government as a petition to recover the cost of damages. All of these cases took years to be resolved and involved tedious and detailed investigations whereby members of the congregation, as well as unbiased witnesses, testified in order to prevent the commission of insurance fraud. The required criteria for granting a claim involved several factors that had to be determined by the panel conducting each investigation. This included a formal declaration that absolved the churches from charges of insurrection and treason for supporting the Confederate States of America. Although each church was eventually granted this absolution, it was most likely given as an amicable political gesture on behalf of the United States government.

The Court of Claims, regarding the case of the *Baptist Church of Fredericksburg Virginia v. the United States* (Case No. 11768 Cong.), presented a deposition taken April 13, 1905, before E.F. Chesley, a notary public. The Statement of Case read:

This is a claim for occupation of and damage to the church building of the Baptist Church of Fredericksburg, Virginia, alleged to have been used and damaged by the *military forces of the United States during the late civil war, stated at $4000.00. The claim was referred to the court February 28, 1905, by resolution of the United States Senate under act of Congress approved March 3, 1887, known as the Tucker Act.*

Fifty years after the end of the War Between the States, the members of the Fredericksburg Baptist Church finally received financial restitution from the Federal government in the amount of $3,000. Damages to the building and its contents included countless bullet and projectile holes, shattered windows, damaged or stolen pews and missing furniture. Books and other items were also destroyed or missing. In lieu of aid from Washington, D.C., most of the area's churches were able to petition funds from Northern churches on their behalf, as well as local pledges from wealthier citizens whose accounts had not been as devastated as their less fortunate brethren. Eventually, in May of 1865, the members of the Fredericksburg Baptist Church were able to resume worship, regain membership and reestablish their influence in the community.

One of the biggest challenges during the immediate postwar period, just prior to Reconstruction, was the resolution of social relationships between the white and black citizens of the town. Although Fredericksburg Baptist Church had once been integrated and helped to establish the African church at Shiloh Baptist, the war had taken its toll on both sides of the race line. Pastor Thomas Dunaway was well aware of the bitterness of defeat among the pro-secessionist members of his congregation, as well as the tension regarding the town's newly freed African population. He addressed both at his denomination's first postwar annual meeting, held in Richmond in June of 1865.

Dunaway joined his peers in adopting a resolution declaring the war finished. It stated, "That whatever may have been our past views, aims, or efforts regarding the issues which have divided the Northern and Southern States, we deem it our duty as patriots and as Christians to accept the order of Providence, yield unreserved and faithful obedience to the 'powers that be,' and to preserve such a course of conduct as shall best promote peace and prosperity of the country."

In addition, a committee report concerning the "religious instruction for colored people" presented at the convention stated, "Our obligation is…unquestionable…Our changed relations to them do not lessen, in any wise, this obligation. They are ignorant and need instruction. They are sinful and need the purifying influence of the gospel, and we shall be culpably inconsistent if, while making efforts to send the message of salvation to Africa, we neglect it among the Africans in our midst." The notion of establishing and maintaining Sunday schools for all freed blacks followed. Shiloh Baptist (Old Site) also returned to rebuild, recover and expand. Together, these two churches, along with another expansion, Shiloh Baptist (New Site), make up the entire Baptist population of Old Town.

Despite the trials and tribulations that plagued the Baptists, Pastor Dunaway witnessed great spiritual and economic recovery among his congregation in the first five years after the war. In a letter written by him for the *Religious Herald* he wrote: "When I took charge of the church…I soon discovered indications that God was ready to pour out His Spirit upon the people. I determined to make a special and protracted effort for the salvation of souls." He closed by saying, "Truly may we say, 'The Lord hath done great things for us, whereof we are glad.' To Him be all the glory now and forever. Amen."

Today

Pastor Dunaway's faith appears to have helped to sustain the Baptist church, as it underwent an extensive rehabilitation of its sanctuary and its congregation. It also helped the church to grow by leaps and bounds. In 1855, there were approximately two hundred church members listed on its rolls. In 2007, the membership stands closer to two thousand. Sometime during the period from 1866 to 1868, workmen disinterred the remains of two Union soldiers at the Baptist church—perhaps from the narrow yard that surrounded it—and moved them to the Fredericksburg National Cemetery, where they were reunited with other fallen comrades. It was a first step toward returning the site to "normal." Since then, Fredericksburg Baptist Church has expanded, adding additions in 1898, 1910, 1950, 1972 and 1990. Today it is the largest church in the entire Historical District of Fredericksburg.

SHILOH BAPTIST CHURCH
(OLD SITE)

I could not begin to express my new born hopes for I felt already like I was certain of my freedom now. I did not know what to say for I was dumb with joy and could only thank God and laugh.
— *Fredericksburg slave John Washington*
reflecting on his escape across the river to the Union camps at Falmouth

Background

Located at 801 Sophia Street, Shiloh Baptist Church was sold to its black congregation by the resident white church for a sum of $500. Shortly after gaining its independence, the African American congregation flourished, building a large membership of both free and slave members. After the Emancipation Proclamation took effect, the congregation appointed its first black pastor, Reverend George Dixon. When the Civil War ended, members who had fled north to escape the fighting returned and the church once again thrived. Today there are two Shiloh Baptist Churches in the Fredericksburg area (Old Site and New Site). During the Civil War, the original Shiloh Church served as a hospital for Union soldiers.

Church Origin

As presented in the previous chapter, Shiloh Baptist Church (Old Site) evolved from the integrated Fredericksburg Baptist Church. The original congregation included both white and black members, and by the 1840s over 75 percent of the eight-hundred-member assembly was black. Not surprisingly, the archived transcripts recalling the division of the church and the sale of its building to the African American membership differ greatly in tone between the two races. This is completely understandable, given the time in American history when they were recorded. Although both churches share a historical bond today, this was not always the case during the racial strife of the pre–civil rights period.

In the late 1800s, the white congregation of Fredericksburg Baptist Church acknowledged the racial tensions leading up to the separation, but presented the split

Shiloh Baptist Church (Old Site). *Courtesy Dawn S. Bowen, PhD.*

as a magnanimous gesture on their part. The African American records, on the other hand, negatively recall the terms of dismissal and financial debates that occurred over the property. Therefore, as the white members' point of view has been outlined in the previous section, the following recollections present the other side of the story, as written by the black congregation.

After growing in numbers for several decades, the Baptists recognized an escalating problem with the space limitations in the old building used as the first Baptist Meeting House. Both white and black members initiated a pledge drive to gain the finances that were necessary to construct a much larger sanctuary. Despite their limited resources when compared to their white counterparts, the African American population subscribed the impressive amount of $1,100 in financial support. As written in the congregation's minutes dated September 28, 1855, the church's "colored brethren and sisters" pledged the sum to assist in the "construction of a new building."

At the time it is said that there were at least 625 African American members at Fredericksburg Baptist Church. This included John Washington, who escaped the bonds of slavery after crossing the Rappahannock River and entering the Union army's encampment, which was located at Falmouth. He then proceeded to Washington, D.C., where many other members of his church had fled and established a new Shiloh Baptist Church in the nation's capital. After the war, he wrote and published a fascinating collection of memoirs detailing his escape in 1862.

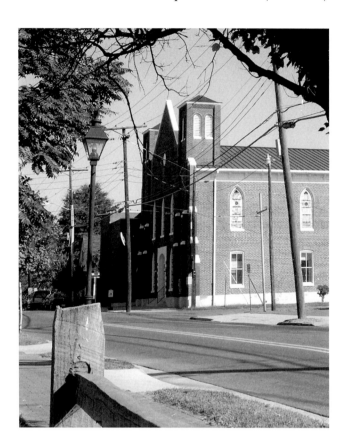

Shiloh Baptist Church (Old Site) today. *Courtesy Shiloh Baptist Church.*

Despite worshiping together for years, tensions between the two races heightened in 1854, nearly ten years before the War Between the States would erupt over states' rights and the institution of slavery. It was at this time that the groups began to worship separately, with the black members meeting on Sunday afternoons as opposed to the mornings. Eventually the idea of building a newer church "in town" for the white congregational members and leaving the riverside building in the hands of the black members was approved. In September of 1855, the church secretary recorded, "It has always been our intention to give up our old house of worship to the colored portion of our church." This decision came on the heels of the pledge drive in which the African Americans had vowed to provide a large gift.

A feud ignited over what financial obligations were to be fulfilled. The white committee members insisted that no property would be officially transferred until the beneficiaries fulfilled their "moral obligation" to make good on all pledges up to the proposed sum of $1,100. After much discussion, a compromise of $500 ($400, according to Fredericksburg Baptist Church accounts) was reached between the two parties. According to the church minutes taken on February 3, 1856:

> *Resolved, that we shall still consider our coloured brethren as part of our church and feel it to be our duty as well as pleasure to aid them in any way we can to build up the cause*

of our divine master and to secure to them the peaceable occupancy of the house they now worship, with all the privileges as a branch of our church which the laws of our state extend to them.

As was often the case during this period, the Caucasian majority frequently took a paternalistic approach to its African American neighbors who were less rooted in recognition of equality and more rooted in the moral obligation to assist those souls held in bondage. Additionally, whites often perceived blacks, especially slaves, to be both ignorant and living in a state of irreligion. In their minds, even slave owners were answering the call to "go forth and make disciples of all nations," which included those who they ironically deprived of the ability to read and write. In essence, the denial of an education in any form prevented blacks from getting out from under the intellectual shadow of the white population.

Racism obviously posed a conflict of conscience for many practicing Christians, as the very same people offering spiritual nurturing to their "coloured brethren" were often slave owners themselves. This represented a paradoxical relationship that existed between devout believers and their servants. The majority of whites appeared to have been benevolent at best about racial equality. Many citizens, even those who opposed the institution of slavery, still did not consider the black population to be equal. To some, the path to freedom for blacks meant colonization. To others, slavery had been ordained by their personal interpretations of Biblical scripture.

However, white supremacy was not embraced by all of Fredericksburg's citizens. A local Presbyterian woman named Mary B.M. Blackford recorded the hypocrisy that she witnessed during worship as well as one minister's efforts to seek colonization for freed blacks. She wrote:

[Slave traders] *have been using the town jail for their purpose, though it is expressly contrary to law, there being no one possessed of moral courage enough to go forward to have this abuse corrected. The town jail faces the Presbyterian Church and I have sat there during the preaching and looked out at the innocent prisoners peeping through the iron bars, and have thought that they were kept there for the crime of designing to be free and to return to those God commanded them to protect and care for. The words would occur to me as I looked around on the worshippers in the Church, "Is not this the fast that I have chosen, to loose the bonds of wickedness, to undo the heavy burdens, and to let the oppressed go free, and that ye break every yoke."*

At the time when my heart was weighed down by watching each day the progress made in building the brick wall that was around the negro jail spoken of above where guiltless prisoners were to be immured, and I looked around in vain for a remedy. (My dear husband did all he could do to stop it.) I was called to the door to see a plain looking country gentleman who wished to see Mr. Blackford on business. I told him Mr. B. would soon be at home and asked him to be seated. On entering into conversation with him, I discovered he had been directed by the good and holy man Father Kobler (a Methodist Preacher) to get advice from my husband as to the steps necessary to be taken to procure

Right: Conception of original building. *Courtesy Shiloh Baptist Church.*

Below: African Baptist and white Baptist churches. *Courtesy U.S. National Park Service.*

African member dismissal rolls.
Courtesy Shiloh Baptist Church.

a passage to Liberia for a young woman, the only Slave he possessed. He told that he was about to remove with his family to Illinois, and he wished to give her her freedom and every advantage. He could have gotten, he told me, four hundred dollars for her in the neighborhood.

This act of disinterestedness cheered me; it was the green spot in the moral desert I had been wandering through. I thank God for showing me just then that there were some who felt for the oppressed; it cheered and refreshed my spirits, and I can better bear to witness the progress of the jail, though I trust I shall never be hardened to such sights. The young woman who was liberated by the gentleman…was sent to town to the care of the Female Colonization Society, and was sent to Liberia by them under the protection of some missionaries who were going to that place. Along with her we sent another freed girl manumitted by Mr. Morton.

Those who endured the pains of the institution of slavery firsthand best presented the deplorable treatment of African Americans held for forced labor. In 1850, a convention of fugitive slaves was held in New York City. One of the country's most outspoken publications on the subject was the *Anti-Slavery Bugle*. On September 28 of that year, the

1854   1864   1914

JUBILEE JOTTINGS

(A jubilee shall the fiftieth year be.—Lev. 25 : 11)

THE SHILOH BAPTIST CHURCH (OLD SITE)

Rev. J. C. DIAMOND, B. D., Pastor

50th ANNIVERSARY AND JUBILEE

Began Worship as a Separate Congregation in 1854

Organized as the Shiloh Baptist Church in 1864

A Brief History of the Church

For nearly one hundred years there has been a Baptist Church on the "Old Site" on Water Street, where the Shiloh Baptist Church (O. S.) now stands. For the first thirty years it was a white church, the members being composed of both white and colored people, and it is said that the colored members were in the majority. At first they worshipped together, but later on the colored members worshipped in the afternoon and Rev. George Rowe, a white minister, the grandfather of the present Mayor of the city, preached for them.

In 1854, the congregation having outgrown the building on Water Street, moved into a new building which had been erected on Princess Anne St. The old building on Water Street was then turned over entirely to the colored people, and Rev. Armistead Walker, one of the first ordained colored ministers in the State, preached for them.

During the war when the Union soldiers occupied the town the church was used as a hospital. The benches were torn out and the property otherwise damaged. The church has a claim in the Omnibus Claim Bill which is now before Congress and there is a chance that it will receive a goodly sum of money from the government in adjustment of its claim.

At the close of the war this congregation organized under the name of the Shiloh Baptist Church, and had for its first pastor, Rev. George Dixon. Nearly all of the older members of the church today were baptized by Rev. George Dixon.

Of the twelve men who banded themselves together after the war, organized the church and began to repair the building ; only one, Bro. "Jim" Coleman, is in the church today. The other eleven are either all dead or have left the city. While the pastor, Rev. Dixon, was away trying to raise the money to replace the pews destroyed by the soldiers, these men remained behind and did what they could to repair the building and get the congregation together.

Rev. L. G. Walden succeeded Rev. Dixon, and he, after a short pastorate, was succeeded by Rev. Willis Robinson. (For a list of the subsequent pastors, see page 8.)

Shiloh Baptist Church anniversary program. *Courtesy U.S. National Park Service.*

Bugle printed a piece to coincide with the convention entitled "Letters to the American Slaves." It stated:

> *So galling was our bondage, that to escape from it, we suffered the loss of all things, and braved every peril, and endured every hardship. Some of us left parents, some wives, some children. Some of us were wounded with guns and dogs, as we fled. Some of us secreted ourselves in the suffocating holds of ships. Nothing was so dreadful to us as slavery.*

Frustrated by the notion of being designated as secondary citizens worshiping at a "branch," the black members of Fredericksburg Baptist petitioned for more independence. In March, the following declaration resolved the matter:

> *Whereas the colored portion of our church have applied to us for the privilege of being constituted into a separate church, and having requested us to appoint a committee to draft a constitution for that purpose, therefore, resolved that we will grant this request on the*

condition that the coloured brethren pledge themselves by a resolution of their body to make good to us the balance of the subscription made by them towards paying for our new house of worship, say the balance of five hundred dollars.

Upon paying the additional sum of $500, the deed to the church was transferred. The original membership rolls on file at the Shiloh Baptist Church (Old Site) outline the legacy of the African American congregation. In the first column are listed the names of each individual who was received into membership in November and December of 1853. The second column records the date on which each member was baptized into the faith. The third column shows the month and year when each member was received by letter as a transfer from another church. The fourth column (mostly empty) presents the month and year that each member was reinstated into the church after being previously removed from membership. The fifth column is the most striking, as it lists the date of "May 4, 1856" over and over as the day on which all of the church's black members were dismissed. This date is significant, as it represents the official split between the races. As the white side of the church "took" the identity of the previously integrated house of worship, the black members were "dismissed" from the official Baptist records. This in turn enabled the newly formed African American Baptist congregation to be received into the denomination as a separate body from that of its predecessors. Both churches were then required to draft new constitutions.

Despite reaching an agreement over the split, another debate developed regarding the legal requirement of a white pastor shepherding the African American church. This concern was addressed in multiple meetings that were recorded. Minutes taken by the white congregation on February of 1856 stated:

Whereas we desire the coloured portion of our church to enjoy the privilege of regular public worship in the house we formerly occupied, therefore, resolved, that the esteemed Brother Elder George Rowe, who has for several months been laboring among them with much acceptance, be requested to continue these labors, and to administer the ordinances of the gospel among them, and also, in conjunction with our pastor, to attend to the order and discipline of the church so long as it may be mutually agreeable to the parties concerned, the coloured brethren being expected to make him such compensation for his services as he and they may agree upon.

George Rowe was an elder in the church and owned seven slaves himself. He had established a familiar rapport with the "coloured congregation" and was well versed in the study and preaching of Biblical scripture. By 1858, Shiloh Baptist Church was blossoming and its numbers continued to increase. Rowe remained in the position of congregational "overseer" until President Lincoln's Emancipation Proclamation took effect. At that time, a longtime and active member of the church named George Dixon was appointed as the first African American pastor.

Unfortunately, a short time later, the entire town was devastated by the battle that raged upon the arrival of the Federal army. This prompted over three hundred members,

Dixon included, to flee north to Washington, where they established a daughter church in a large horse stable christened Shiloh Baptist of Washington, D.C. This church is still in operation today. Those who remained in Fredericksburg met sporadically in homes and an old warehouse on Fifteenth Street. Unfortunately, the church building was counted among the structural casualties of the Battle of Fredericksburg.

The War and Reconstruction

Many of the black churches in the South were abandoned throughout the course of the Civil War. As towns across Virginia switched possession repeatedly between the defending Confederate forces and invading Union troops, black citizens often found themselves caught in the middle. As slaves, they were either hiding from the posses hired by local plantation owners to gather them up, or attempting to make their escape to the North. Aid in this venture was sometimes provided by the occupying Federal troops. At other times, the refugees were looked down upon as an unwanted burden to soldiers on the march. Armies that were barely able to take care of themselves did not welcome the additional responsibilities of caring for contraband.

Therefore it is difficult, if not nearly impossible, to find members' credible, firsthand accounts of Fredericksburg's nearby engagements. Simply stated, the majority of the congregational members were absent at the time that these events occurred. Perhaps the best recollections of their experiences during the engagement come from the post–Reconstruction era testimonies of witnesses for the Court of Claims investigations conducted by the United States government in 1904. Military accounts seldom refer specifically to the African Baptist church, and most postwar recollections are either vague or incomplete. During the war, when the Union forces occupied the town, their meetinghouse was used as a stable, a barracks and later a field hospital. As a result, the benches were torn out and the walls and flooring were extensively damaged. The exterior also suffered damage during the initial bombardment and subsequent mêlée.

After the conflict ended, the church was reorganized under the name Shiloh Baptist and was officiated by the returning pastor, Reverend George Dixon. He was a former slave of Mrs. Meade Thornton of Caroline County who had purchased his freedom in 1856. In addition to preaching in Spotsylvania, the July 26, 1890 edition of the *Star* listed in the "Colored Churches" history section that Reverend Dixon was also preaching at another church that he helped to organize in Caroline at the time.

Another black preacher, the Reverend J.E. Brown, was also listed in the same paper as a "pastor of the 'old site' church." It reported that he was born in Bedford County and had been a slave of Colonel Robert C. Allen. The article went on to outline the path that Brown took then toward becoming an ordained minister. It stated:

> He soon afterwards entered the ministry, and after seven years work in this calling he retired, and entered the Richmond Theological Seminary, where he graduated, and re-entered the ministry and accepted the pastoral charge of a church in Chesterfield, where

Shiloh Baptist Church (circa 1920s). *Courtesy Shiloh Baptist Church (Old Site).*

"Colored" teamsters in the Union army. *Courtesy National Archives.*

he remained for fifteen years, when he accepted a call to the church here, in 1887, which
has greatly prospered under his ministry, the membership now numbering 404.

The article went on to add that he had baptized, during his ministry, over one thousand people and that both whites and blacks respected him—an interesting distinction to mention that certainly speaks to the times. It appears that singling someone out for being accepted by both races was an accolade.

Returning to the months immediately following the war, one of the first goals of the newly established Shiloh congregation was to join its white peers in submitting a claim, using the Omnibus Claim Bill, which enabled Southerners to petition for financial reimbursement for damage inflicted on their properties due to the actions of the Federal army. As outlined in the previous chapter, this involved a long and meticulous process, which involved detailed witness testimonies and cross-examinations.

The testimony of four gentlemen, including the Reverend George L. Dixon from Shiloh Baptist Church, outlined eyewitness accounts of the experiences of the church during the battle and its aftermath. *THE COURT OF CLAIMS of Trustees of Shiloh (old site) Baptist Church of Fredericksburg Va., v. The United States* (Case No. 11781 Cong.) presented the deposition taken on July 29, 1904. The claim was for a sum of $3,000, including reimbursement for $900 worth of repair costs that had already been incurred by the church. The Statement of Case read:

> *This is a claim for use of and damage to the church building of Shiloh (old site) Baptist*
> *Church, of Fredericksburg, Virginia, by the military forces of the United States during*
> *the late civil war, stated at $3000.00. The claim was referred to the court February 28,*
> *1905, by resolution of the United States Senate under act of Congress approved March*
> *3, 1887, known as the Tucker Act.*

The Abstract of Evidence recorded the testimonies of Shiloh's representatives. The first witness to take the stand was a longtime church member named George Triplett who presented his firsthand knowledge of the Union soldiers' conduct and resultant damage. Unlike many of his comrades, Triplett "stuck it out" and remained in the area as the fighting raged on around him. He stated:

> *The Union Army occupied the church December, 1862. At that time they used the*
> *basement to put their horses in and the upper part was used for the soldiers to stay in.*
> *They then occupied it for sometime while Grant was operating in the Wilderness, using it*
> *for a hospital. During this occupation they took out all the windows and all the pews, and*
> *knocked out the pillars, and by taking out the pillars the corner of the building afterward*
> *fell out. They also took the seats out of the gallery and the steps leading up to the same.*
> *They also knocked the side off the gallery; the ceiling was all knocked down and we had*
> *to have it plastered. Burnside's troops occupied the building in 1862, and the second time*
> *it was Grant's troops.*

Triplett's associate, Thomas Dennis, gave a much more detailed summary of the Federal army's presence at the church. Although he wasn't a member of the congregation, his witness of the events surrounding the damaging of the building that stood a few blocks from his home proved to be valuable testimony. Due to his location in town, one may assume that Mr. Dennis was a white citizen who may have been able to observe the events both prior to and shortly after the occupation ended. Upon inspection of Shiloh Baptist Old Site's handwritten membership rolls, as well as the U.S. Census of free inhabitants of 1860, no "Dennis" appeared in any form, reinforcing the notion that no family member attended the church either. Therefore, the witness must have been called as an unbiased outsider. He testified:

> *The Union troops used the building for a hospital and put their horses in the basement. They used the building when Hooker was here and then they used it for some four or five months when Grant was here. They tore up the floors, knocked out the windows, took the pews and almost destroyed the inside of the church. They also took out some of the pillars under the basement part, which later caused one end to fall out of the building and the church had to be rebuilt.*

Each church in this book was found to exhibit loyalty to the Union in the Summary Statement of each case, but Shiloh Baptist Church (Old Site) may be the only one that truly deserved that distinction. Clearly, the white congregation would have most likely supported the Confederacy, as so many of its clergy and loved ones were serving in the field. An African church, however, no matter how peacefully it was coexisting with white society, would not have been as enthusiastic in supporting a cause that intended to preserve the institution of bondage over its membership. Additionally, as a colored congregation, many of the members fled north following the initial occupation of the town. Any support of the wartime effort would have most likely been as Federal wagon teamsters, stretcher bearers and even soldiers in the "Negro regiments."

Ironically, it was the African Baptist church that received only 50 percent of the monies petitioned ($1,500) from the government, while many of the neighboring white churches received close to the full amount claimed. This proved to be just one more example of the many civil rights hardships that confronted black Southerners for another one hundred years. Despite winning their freedom, African Americans were called upon to meet additional challenges, as Jim Crow laws and segregation stifled their independence and equality in the post–Civil War South.

One site that testifies to the sacrifice for racial equality is the cemetery, where those who fell so that other men could be free were laid to rest. On Memorial Day 2006, the Reverend Lawrence A. Davies, pastor of Shiloh Baptist Church (Old Site), gave a powerful address at the Fredericksburg National Cemetery. In it he stated the significance of this special resting place for both black and white descendants:

> *Fredericksburg National Cemetery was created immediately after the Civil War, between 1866 and 1868. Not surprisingly, it was Fredericksburg's African American*

population—the newly freed slaves—that first embraced this hallowed ground. As early as the mid and late 1860s, African Americans journeyed to Fredericksburg to decorate the graves of the Union dead with flowers. Former slaves came by the hundreds from places as far away as Washington, D.C., and Richmond. They came to pay homage to those who had made the supreme sacrifice in order that they may be free.

For black citizens, Fredericksburg National Cemetery was a tangible reminder of their newfound liberty. For that reason, their ceremonies contained an element of joy that whites could not understand. A Northern veteran noted with some perplexity that Memorial Day was regarded as a gala day by African Americans. He could not understand the former slaves' joy because he had not experienced their bondage. He took freedom for granted.

The reverend also reflected on the annual pilgrimages to the cemetery that were made by many members of the African American community from all over the country. He recalled how they came together at his church and formed a long procession line that marched up Lafayette Boulevard to the center of the cemetery. Often a band dressed in black and playing traditional music for the occasion accompanied them. In 1871, when Union veterans first began to arrive in Fredericksburg hoping to pay homage to their fallen comrades, they were shunned by the local white Confederate sympathizers, but embraced by the African American contingent.

The editor of the *Fredericksburg Ledger* expressed the view of the town's white citizens in those early days following the end of the war. He wrote:

How does the case differ here? Who are these "heroes" whose graves you invite into this community, white and black, unitedly, to "honor"? Are they not some of them, the men who bombarded and destroyed one half of Fredericksburg, who sacked our houses, who profaned and polluted our homes and firesides and most sacred relics of the past, who robbed us, and even destroyed what they could not steal, who desecrated our alters and our churches, in which we had worshipped since childhood? Did they not overwhelm us at last by more "brute force of numbers" after the Confederates, man for man, had whipped and destroyed them two to one? All these things are history and will not be denied by any but the ignorant or the depraved.

Fortunately, as the years of the Civil War began to fade further and further into the past, relations between the North's and South's veterans began to mend. As a result, the hallowed grounds that surround the city became more than just historical markers. They became memorials to the seeds of reconciliation that were sown. Even more symbolic was the fact that the land, where brother was pitted against brother, had become a tangible reminder of the cost endured for liberty and freedom for all Americans. No one appreciated this sacrifice more than the members of Shiloh Baptist Church (Old Site), whose tale of perseverance and courage in the face of adversity has been shared and admired for generations.

Today

At the dawning of the twenty-first century, Shiloh Baptist Church (Old Site) continues to thrive in the Fredericksburg community. Over the last decade, many structural repairs and additions have been made to the historic building that still stands near the river on Sophia Street. In 2003, the entire top of the 1890 building was removed, including the ceiling and the roof. A new roof was built, allowing for a higher ceiling in the sanctuary, thus providing a more spacious feeling, especially in the balcony, which was originally used by blacks only in the integrated Baptist meetinghouse. In 2004, the church celebrated its 200th anniversary and commemorated the event by refurbishing the classic 1925 pipe organ that is still in service today.

St. George's
Episcopal Church

Orders came to withdraw the pickets from Fredericksburg. I was in the church steeple, and had been forgotten. When I came down at night, and went to my old position in the rifle pits, I found that my whole company was gone. I was holding the town myself.
—Union soldier left behind on post in St. George's bell tower

Background

Located at the corner of 905 Princess Anne and George Streets, the settlement's original church was built by Colonel Henry Willis in 1732. The current Roman Revival–style structure was built in 1849 and is the third church to be constructed on the premises. Colonel John Spotswood, son of the colonial governor, donated the church's original bell in 1751. (It was later replaced in 1788 and again in 1856.) The Fredericksburg City Council placed a clock in the bell tower in 1851. During the Battle of Fredericksburg, the church survived many artillery strikes. It also served as a meeting place for the Confederate officers and a hospital for wounded Union soldiers. In 1995, the congregation celebrated its 275th anniversary and continues to function as one of the largest churches in the area. The green spire of St. George's steeple stands out today as the tallest marker in the city's skyline.

Church Origin

St. George's Episcopal Church has several rather unique distinctions that set it apart from the other congregations of Fredericksburg. Foremost, it was the first church that was established at the original settlement of Germanna in 1720 as St. George's Parish by the House of Burgesses of colonial Virginia. Eight years later, the assembly formally established the city of Fredericksburg, Virginia. Therefore, St. George's is the only church in the entire city to be actually mandated by English rule. At the time of its construction, this primitive house of worship was designated to serve the residents of the original frontier port city. As the settlement grew, so did the church.

St. George's Episcopal Church. *Courtesy Dawn S. Bowen, PhD.*

According to Paula S. Felder's study, titled *Forgotten Companions: The First Settlers of Spotsylvania County and Fredericksburgh Town (With Notes on Early Land Use)*, the Church of England's history in Virginia is one fraught with personal conflict. It stated:

> *The Protestant Reformation which swept Europe in the sixteenth century took a different course in England, principally because of the marital problems of King Henry VIII. Determined to divorce his first wife, who had produced no male heir, Henry sought Papal dispensation to nullify his marriage. His quarrel with the Catholic Church became a jurisdictional conflict in which he sought to assert the authority of the state against the supernational church. In 1533, Parliament passed the Acts of Appeals, which cut the legal ties between the English Church and the Papacy; and in 1534, Henry was declared supreme head of the Church of England, the legally established form of Christianity in England.*
>
> *The first colonists in Virginia brought with them the canon (church) law of the Established Church as well as the common law of England. As there was no bishop in the colony, the church came under the legislative authority of the General Assembly as*

St. George's Episcopal Church

St. George's Episcopal Church today. *Courtesy St. George's Episcopal Church.*

Seating Plan of St George's Church in 1849

Front (along top):

Left side:
- 4 Mrs. J. D. Taylor — $350
- 3 J. B. Ficklen — $450
- 2 Mrs. Coalter / Chs. Herndon — $460
- 1 Rector

Center: Desk | Pulpit | Desk — Table — Chancel
Pews Sold April 23d, 1849 — Church partially burnt, July 1854

Right side:
- 100 T. B. Barton — $405
- 99 R. W. Carter — $380
- 98 J. T. Lamay — $355
- 97 Mrs. Hunter — $310

Communion Rail

#	Name	Name	#
5	J. Coakely $315	Capt Hamilton $385	72
6	M. H. Crump $295	Dr. J. B. Hall $395	70
7	A. Goodwin $295	M. Forbes $400	68
8	Mrs. J. R. Harrison $320	D. H. Gordon $405 / C. Wistar Wallace	66
9	Thos. Pratt $310	Misses Fitzhugh $415	64
10	M. Slaughter $325	Dr. J. H. Wallace $400 / A. W. W.	62
11	Mrs. V. Carmichael $245	W. K. Gordon $400 / Dr. A. G. Doggett	60
12	Mrs. A. S. Hayes $275	H. Fitzhugh $385	58
13	Dr. B. S. Herndon $290	T. F. Knox $370	56
14	Mrs. J. B. Gray $290	T. F. Knox $370	54
15	Dr. J. Cooke $280	Dr. J. G. Wallace $360	52
16	W. C. I. Rothrock / Robt. Hall $230	Dr. J. R. Taylor $340	50
17	F. J. Wiatt $255	Y. Smith $325 / J. Z. Stansbury	48
18	W. R. Mason, Jr. $240	Y. Smith $325 / Dr. W. M. Smith	46
19	J. W. Johnston $230	Dr. Carmichael $300	44
20	N. Fitzhugh $225	J. J. Berry $280	42
21	Jane H. Dickinson $225	R. D. Minor $255	40
22	Mrs. Ellis	Paul Clay $255	38
		$200 Buck	

#	Name	Name	#
73	R. C. L. Moncure $310	Dr. Wm. Browne $340	96
71	Miss Agnes Gray / St. G. R. Fitzhugh $390	P. Goolrick $275	95
69	Mrs. Scott / Dr. Wm. S. Scott $385	Geo. B. Scott $280	94
67	Mrs. F. Scott / Mrs. Allen $385	Dr. H. Morson $295	93
65	J. F. Scott / J. P. Corbin $400	A. K. Phillips $300	92
63	Hugh Scott / B. S. Herndon $400	Benj. Temple $290 / A. B. Botts	91
61	S. Phillips $370	W. S. Barton $245 / A. B. Botts, Sr.	90
59	Jno. Hart $360	C. S. Scott $245	89
57	Miss Jane Hart / E. M. Braxton $360	H. B. Hoomes $265	88
55	Jno. L. Chinn $355	Misses Pearson $265	87
53	Wm. Pollock $330	W. H. Cunningham $255	86
51	Capt. J. Rudd $325	J. J. Young $230	85
49	J. M. Whittemore $300	T. H. Botts $225	84
47	F. Slaughter $290	Duff Green $225	83
45	J. W. Lucas $300	Miss Goodwin $225	82
43	J. H. Roberts / F. W. Johnston $270	Dr. Mason $225	81
41	M. A. Blankman $245	J. Galleher $225	80
39	Mrs. A. J. Fitzhugh $225	Jno. Minor $200	79
		Mrs. Smock	78

Where there is a lower name on a pew, it is generally that of a subsequent purchaser.

Church seating plan, circa 1849. *Courtesy St. George's Episcopal Church.*

Above left: Tower panorama: east-northeast view. *Courtesy U.S. National Park Service.*

Above right: Tower panorama: north view. *Courtesy U.S. National Park Service.*

Above left: Tower panorama: northeast view. *Courtesy U.S. National Park Service.*

Above right: Tower panorama: northwest view. *Courtesy U.S. National Park Service.*

early as 1689. Many years later, in 1869, the Bishop of London appointed the Reverend James Blair to serve as his representative or Commissary. Blair became a powerful figure, founder and president of the College of William and Mary. But even in fulfilling his responsibilities for representing the Church, he functioned through secular channels as a member of the Governor's Council.

Above left: Tower panorama: southeast view. *Courtesy U.S. National Park Service.*

Above right: Tower panorama: south-southeast view. *Courtesy U.S. National Park Service.*

Above left: Tower panorama: south-southwest view. *Courtesy U.S. National Park Service.*

Above right: Tower panorama: southwest view. *Courtesy U.S. National Park Service.*

Along with the English church came English rules and regulations. Many of the punishments for breaking the covenants of the church were also brought over from England to the New World. This included myriad public ridicules and non-lethal tortures, which were used to enforce both civic and congregational codes. The Act of Assembly in 1705 established a strict list of "Religious Offenses" and appropriate punishments. The offenses included: the willful absence from attending church services for over a month; failure to conduct oneself in a decent and orderly manner while in

Above left: Tower panorama: west view. *Courtesy U.S. National Park Service.*

Above right: Tower panorama: west-southwest view. *Courtesy U.S. National Park Service.*

church; participating in any disorderly meeting; gaming or tippling on the Sabbath day; making a casual journey or travel upon the road other than to and from church on the Sabbath; and finally, working in the fields, stores or any other labor calling on the Sabbath.

The punishment for these "crimes" varied from a fine of five shillings or fifty pounds of tobacco for each offense, to ten lashes on the bare back. More serious offenses, such as adultery, were punishable by time in the public stocks and severe fines up to one thousand pounds of tobacco and cask. There was also a rule condemning the act of religious dissention that was drafted in an obscure act of Parliament passed in 1689, although it has been recorded that other religious groups may have existed outside of the Church of England at the time. Historian Robert Beverly discovered accounts of what appeared to be three small Quaker groups and two smaller Presbyterian groups coexisting with St. George's in 1705. Spotsylvania County court records dated June 1, 1742, present a case in which Henry Brock (religion not provided) had charges against him dismissed after it was proven that he was not a dissenter of the Church of England, but another denomination's practitioner.

Despite its strict code of conduct and ties back to England, St. George's prospered and grew into a bustling church in early Virginia. During the colonial period, the church was responsible for the health and welfare of orphans, widows and the sick. It also assisted the poor and downtrodden. As a spiritually educating pillar in the community, St. George's also established male and female charity schools, as well as Sunday schools for black children.

When the newest church building was constructed, the box pews were sold or rented to the families for a monthly subscription fee. These funds went to cover the cost of the

Church minute remarks on battle. *Courtesy St. George's Episcopal Church.*

facility as well as day-to-day church operations. The names of many of these original members are still engraved on the pew doors. This resulted in the equivalent of assigned or reserved seating at every service, thus making it fairly easy to keep track of individual member attendance, even in a sanctuary as large as St. George's.

Throughout the mid- to late 1700s, members and friends of the Washington family begin attending services at St. George's Church. This included William Paul, brother to America's father of naval warfare, Commodore John Paul Jones, as well as George Washington's brother Charles and brother in-law Fielding Lewis, who also served the church as a vestryman. Jones would not be the only congregational member with famous military ties, as blood ancestors of the World War II hero General George Patton also attended the church. Several of them are buried in the adjacent cemetery.

Following the Revolutionary War and victory for America's independence, the country's church-state ties were dissolved and the denomination was incorporated into the newly formed Episcopal Church of the United States. Unfortunately, this was not the only war to touch St. George's, as another fight over independence came knocking at its door.

Old Communion Set Taken In War, Finally Restored

Cup, Last of Four Pieces to Be Returned, Has Just Been Received By St. George's Episcopal Church. Was Given to Church in 1827. Found In the North.

The return just the other day to St. George's Episcopal Church of a Communion cup which has been missing nearly sixty-nine years, concludes the restoration of a complete Communion set presented to church in 1827 and which was stolen from the edifice during the Civil War. In the original set were four separate pieces. They wandered far afield before their return, but three of pieces were returned some years ago, two at one time and the other at another time.

The whereabouts of the fourth piece was unknown until a few weeks ago when the Rev. Dudley Boogher, rector of the church, received a communication from Mrs. L. A. Thayer, of Wollaston, Massachusetts, stating that she had in her possession a silver communion cup, which had come to her through relatives, with the following inscription engraved on it: "Presented by John Gray, Esq., to the Episcopal Church, St. George's Parish, Fredericksburg, Virginia, A. D. 1827."

Will Be Used Next Sunday.

This cup she offered to return, if the church was still in existence, and the authorities were willing to offer her a suitable reward. Negotiations were at once entered into and on Monday, June 22nd, the

Communion Cup Returned To Local Church.

Stolen communion cup article. *Courtesy St. George's Episcopal Church.*

The War

The archives housed at the Fredericksburg/Spotsylvania National Military Park Service and local Virginia historical societies hold a magnificent array of information pertaining to the landmark churches of Fredericksburg and Spotsylvania County. Clearly, no church appears to have more transcripts on file than that of St. George's Episcopal Church. What is extremely interesting is the large quantity of letters collected from Union soldiers and local slave narratives that paint a magnificent portrait of this particular congregation. St. George's appears to have the distinction of not only being

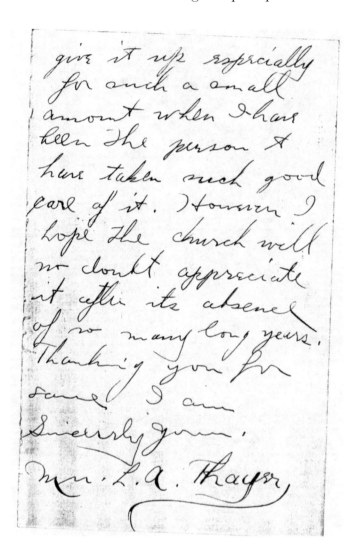

give it up especially for such a small amount when I have been the person & have taken such good care of it.) However, I hope the church will no doubt appreciate it after its absence of so many long years. Thanking you for same, I am Sincerely yours,

Mrs. L. A. Thayer

Letter from cup holder to church. *Courtesy St. George's Episcopal Church.*

one of the few churches that was used extensively by Confederate officers (in addition to the occupying Federal forces), but also one of the first churches to actively incorporate newly freed African Americans in the decade following the end of the Civil War.

Even before the inauguration of secession, St. George's was already playing a part in the public discussions over the matter. In December of 1860, the Young Men's Christian Association used the facility for a public prayer meeting. According to the December 22, 1860 edition of the *Weekly Advertiser*: "For the purpose of making supplication to Almighty God to consider our country's distracted state and preserve the Union amidst the anarchy that now prevails."

In the coming months, tension mounted in Fredericksburg as Union troops attended a service at St. George's Church while staying in the town during the spring of 1862. One of the soldiers recalled:

St. George's Episcopal Church clock tower today. *Courtesy of the author.*

St. George's Episcopal Church
stained-glass window. *Courtesy of*
the author.

On Sunday the eighteenth of May, we attended St. George's…The Rector was the
Reverend Alfred M. Rudolph, a sincere secessionist. He omitted the prayer for the
President of the United States, and it was the first and only time we ever knew him to be
omitted from a service. Mr. Randolph did not pray for the President of the Confederate
States, an omission which, I have no doubt was owing to the presence of U.S. officers in
his church, and Federal troops in his city.

Like the rest of its community, the bombardment of the town by Federal artillery in
December of 1862 had a profound effect on the church and its congregation. As one

of the tallest and most distinctive structures in all of Fredericksburg, St. George's was particularly threatened by Union cannoneers that were positioned at Stafford Heights, on the bluff just behind the stately Chatham Manor. The towering green steeple became a target for the gunners and the structure would eventually be hit over twenty-five times during the course of the battle. A Union artillerist recalled a comrade's attempt to destroy the church's clock: "An officer of another battery remarked that the first shot he put into the city should pass through the clock; in fact, he proposed to breach the wall in such a way that the clock would fall into the body of the church. He explained that he felt impelled to this act through a sense of predestined responsibility."

Another soldier recalled the tremendous barrage that followed: "At 5 A.M. the ball opened by a tremendous cannonade from about 140 guns posted on the high banks of the river…A rebel signal flag was waving from one of the Church steeples, and several shells were directed at and struck the steeple, and the flag disappeared."

Following the battle at Fredericksburg, as well as Chancellorsville and Spotsylvania, St. George's was commandeered for use as a Federal field hospital. According to eyewitness accounts, the entire sanctuary was used to house "both the wounded and dying." Soldiers were carried in through the foyer and put on boards that were laid across the pews. The padded chairs and benches in the altar area were reserved for officers. Candles were used for lighting and army surgeons, nurses and citizens did what they could to give aid and comfort to soldiers from both sides. At all times a provost marshal's patrol attempted to maintain order, in hopes of curbing the crime spree that had begun with the initial arrival of Federal forces.

One theft that was not detected by law enforcement agents resulted in one of the most famous stories surrounding St. George's Episcopal Church: the story of the stolen communion set. In 1827, Mr. John Gray, Esquire, presented a very special communion collection to the church in appreciation of its charity and ministry. During the chaos that ensued following the shelling, invasion and occupation of Fredericksburg, Yankee soldiers, who looted much of the town before their commanders were able to secure order, stole this specially engraved set that had been hidden in the church's rafters. According to an article titled "Old Communion Set Taken In War" printed in the local newspapers, the pieces were then separated and taken north.

Following the conclusion of the conflict, several pieces were hastily located and identified by their engravings. The companion cup and flagon were quickly returned to the church, thanks to the persistence and efforts of the Reverend Maurey, the rector of St. George's parish at the time. The paten, which held the bread in the Holy Communion service, was also detected years later at a pawnshop in New York City. The central piece of the collection, a silver wine chalice, remained missing for sixty-nine years.

In 1931, the whereabouts of the fourth and final piece remained an unsolved mystery, until a communication was sent to the Reverend Dudley Boogher from Mrs. L.A. Thayer of Wollaston, Massachusetts. In a letter, Ms. Wollaston stated that she had in her possession a silver communion chalice that had come to her from a relative with ties to the Union army. She added that the cup had a personalized inscription that read, "Presented by John Gray. Esq., to the Episcopal Church, St. George's Parish,

Fredericksburg, VA A.D. 1827." She then offered to return the cup if, in fact, the church was still in existence and they were able to offer her a suitable reward. After several negotiations, as well as the threat of involving the authorities to recover the "stolen property," the chalice was rightfully returned to St. George's parish on June 22, 1931. The cup appeared to be in perfect condition and was used for communion service the following Sunday, much to the delight of the congregation, which had been anticipating the return of the entire set since it first went missing in 1862.

Despite the perils of the church during the Battle of Fredericksburg in December of 1862, Confederate soldiers reclaimed the premises the following March and used it for a massive religious revitalization that was sweeping across the Southern forces. As the war progressed, a movement referred to as the Great Revival took place in the South. Beginning in 1863, this event was in full progress throughout the Army of Northern Virginia. Before the revival was interrupted by U.S. Grant's attack in May 1864, approximately seven thousand soldiers, composing 10 percent of Lee's force, were reportedly converted. Dr. Gardiner H. Shattuck Jr., author of *A Shield and Hiding Place: The Religious Life of the Civil War Armies*, reported that the "best estimates of conversions in the Union forces place the figure between 100,000 and 200,000 men; about five to ten percent of all individuals engaged in the conflict. In the smaller Confederate Army, at least 100,000 were converted. Since these numbers included only 'conversions' and did not represent the number of soldiers actually swept up in the revivals, which was a more substantial figure, the impact of revivals during the Civil War surely was tremendous."

One of the participating ministers and author of the critically acclaimed studies *Christ In The Camp* and *Religion In The Confederate Army*, Reverend William Jones, DD, recalled his experiences in his memoirs:

> *Long before the appointed hour the spacious Episcopal church, kindly tended by its rector, is filled—nay, packed—to its utmost capacity—lower floor, galleries, aisles, chancel, pulpit steps and vestibule—while hundreds turn disappointed away, unable to find even standing room…I remember that I preached to this vast congregation the very night before Hooker crossed the river, bringing the battles of Second Fredericksburg and Chancellorsville—that, in my closing appeal, I urged them to accept Christ then and there, because they did not know but that they were hearing their "last invitation," and that sure enough we were aroused before the day the next morning by the crossing of the enemy.*
>
> *There were over 500 professions of conversion in these meetings at Fredericksburg, and good work extended out into the neighboring brigades, and went graciously on—only temporarily interrupted by the battle of Chancellorsville—until we took up the line of march for Gettysburg.*

In a personal letter written by Dr. Harry Lovell, who served with the Confederate army and was present in March of 1863, local citizens and soldiers alike benefited greatly by the presence of this much-needed revival. To his sweetheart, Ellen Robie, the doctor wrote:

For the last week or two there has been a good revival going on at the Episcopal Church. Several in which there were a great many soldiers received into the church and baptized. The city presents a baleful appearance. There is no estimating the suffering caused by the shelling of the place. There are hundreds of men who were yard lively who are now reduced to beggary. The poor women and children are starving in every quarter. It is or ought to be a shame in any nation to create such suffering.

Later in the spring, Federal forces once again entered the city, much to the dismay of its shell-shocked citizens. The Reverend Alfred Magill Randolph, rector of St. George's, wrote to his wife from Richmond describing the renewed plight of Fredericksburg's townsfolk:

Richmond
May 6th 1863

My Darling Sallie,

Owing to the condition of the RR and the dread of Yankee Cavalry who are thought to be between here and Ashland trains have not yet been allowed to go to Fredbg—One is expected to go this morning—if so I will go—I am very anxious about our boys—I see that several of Gen Jackson's staff fell killed or wounded at the time he was wounded— names are not given—we learn, too, that Early's division had the hardest fighting to do in front of Fredbg and I cannot leave here until I hear from them—it would be duty to them or to Ma—From what I gather the rectory is complete and the Yankee Army beaten and broken, but with terrible loss on our side—

Our old town has again been occupied for two days by the enemy and I suppose suffered as before—I have heard as yet nothing from individual friends in the army—

God bless you my precious—
Kiss Rob and little sister—
love to all around you

yr own husband
AM Randolph

Less than one year later, in April of 1864, Reverend Randolph recalled preaching to a large congregation in the upper part of the crippled church. Despite all of the damage and destruction in the downtown area, citizens still managed to traipse through the rubble in order to take communion at periodic Sunday services that were conducted by the reverend and no one else. Attendance at these impromptu services fluctuated from two to three hundred people, and soldiers were sometimes present. Reverend Randolph noted that the possibility of his entire congregation returning to the town in the near future was highly improbable, as provisions were so scarce and the threat of reoccupation remained constantly on the minds of those staying behind.

Like many Southern cities, Fredericksburg changed hands on a number of occasions throughout the course of the Civil War. As a result, the churches in town were used by both Confederate and Federal forces as field hospitals and headquarters. Despite their differing allegiances, both sides shared the same perceptions about the horrific sights that they witnessed within the walls of these sacred institutions. However, as they experienced more casualties within the city limits, the Northern soldiers' perspectives read as exceptionally gruesome. Major St. Clair Mulholland of the 116th Pennsylvania "Irish Brigade" wrote a detailed account of the pain and suffering he observed. It is now believed that Major Mulholland may have actually been stationed in the Baptist church and mistakenly quoted his location as the Episcopal chapel. Due to the fog of war that often accompanied a battle, as well as the unfamiliarity with the town, some Union doctors' memories are understandably debatable. Despite this, Mulholland's testimony is no less vivid in his recollection of the horrors that he had observed:

> In the lecture room of the Episcopal church eight operating tables were in full blast, the floor was densely packed with men whose limbs were crushed, fractured and torn. Lying there in deep pools of blood, they waited very patiently; there was no grumbling, no screaming, hardly a moan, many of the badly hurt were smiling, and chatting, and one—who had both legs shot off—was cracking jokes with an officer who could not laugh at the humorous sallies, for his lower jaw was shot away. The cases here were nearly all capital, and amputation was almost always resorted to. Hands and feet, arms and legs were thrown under each table, and the sickening piles grew larger as the night progressed. The delicate limbs of the drummer boy fell along with the rough hand of the veteran in years, but all, every one, was brave and cheerful. Towards morning the conversation flagged, many dropped off to sleep before they could be attended to, and many of them never woke again. Finally the only sound heard was the crunching of the surgeons' saws and now and then the melancholy music of a random shell dismally wailing overhead. Few the prayers that were said, but the soft voice of a boyish soldier as he was lifted on the table, his limbs a mass of quivering, lacerated flesh, was heard as he quietly said "O my God, I offer all my sufferings in atonement for the sins by which I have crucified Thee."

With no space inside the hall, the dead and dying were often stacked in the courtyard just outside the Episcopal church. One wounded soldier recalled, "I walked outside to the street and saw dead soldiers piled on either side as high as the top step, and the fence hanging full of belts, cartridge boxes, canteens, and haversacks." As was customary at the time, temporary burials were conducted with the intentions of later moving the deceased to more suitable and proper gravesites. Often crude markers were used to identify the dead. With over 600,000 people killed during the War Between the States, it was virtually impossible to keep track of them all. Many families were able to recover their loved ones and bring them home for a family burial. Countless others, however, were never able to reunite with their loved ones or achieve closure. According to records obtained by the National Park Service, the remains of thirteen Union soldiers were carefully removed from the St. George's cemetery after the war:

Ambrose, Robert I.	108th New York Infantry	KIA: 1863
Brown, James K.	7th West Virginia Infantry	KIA: 1862
Burnt, John	20th Massachusetts Infantry	KIA: ?
Dermitt, William	12th New Jersey Infantry	KIA: 1863
Faust, A.	106th Pennsylvania Infantry	KIA: ?
G----R, H.	5th Michigan Infantry	KIA: 1862
Hadrian, G.	82nd New York Infantry	KIA: 1863
Lewis, W.H.	1st Delaware Infantry	KIA: 1862
Mc Donald, Daniel	6th New York Artillery	KIA: 1864
Miller, Charles	14th Connecticut Infantry	KIA: 1863
Ray, Charles H.	15th Massachusetts Infantry	KIA: 1863
Watson, Edward	14th Indiana Infantry	KIA: 1862
Webb, John	1st Delaware Infantry	KIA: 1862

Along with its neighboring congregations, St. George's Episcopal Church also made claims for war damages to the Federal government under the Tucker Act of 1887. Its petition demanded a reimbursement of $2,487 for "pews, cushions, and carpeting… alleged to have been appropriated by the United States for the benefit of its wounded soldiers." Unfortunately, St. George's, unlike its neighbors, would never receive a complete payment for these losses. In addition, this church appears to be the only one not to have participated in the inquiry that was sent down from Washington to verify each claimant, as there are no records on file at the National Park archives of such an investigation.

Reconstruction

Two extraordinary slave narratives that were published in the years following the war outlined both the pre- and postwar experiences of African Americans in the Episcopal church. One was titled *Memorys of the Past* and was an autobiographical memoir of John Washington, a former slave. It described his life from 1838 to 1862 in various places in Virginia, especially Fredericksburg. Included was a description of the capture of Fredericksburg by Union troops, his subsequent emancipation and his work as an aide to General Rufus King. The account ended with his removal to Washington, D.C., in 1862.

Washington, who later attended Shiloh Baptist Church (Old Site), recalled his early introduction to Christianity at St. George's Church upon the insistence of his master. In chapter 5 of his memoirs he recalled:

The Episcopal Church in Fredericksburg is situated on the northeast corner of Princess Ann and George Street surrounded on the north and east by the graveyard, Fronting on Princess Ann Street about midway the square was a small one story brick in which I used to go to a Sunday School Sunday afternoon and was taught the catechism and verses of the Bible were read to us by heart. I do not think much good resulted from this school for we was not permitted to learn A.B.C. or to spell. But Mrs. Taliaferro was most zealous in sending me to each such places on Sundays as she would by this means know where I was by asking Miss Olive Hanson, My teacher, by the way she was a most kind and gentle lady and I often think of her sweet face and blue ey[e]s, and feel a spark of gratitude for the efforts on her part, for I really know she would have learned me to read and write if the law had permitted her so to do.

Washington's impressions of St. George's Church during the prewar era certainly stand in contrast to those recorded several years after the war. Clearly over the next decade or so a major change occurred in the Episcopate's perception of emancipated African Americans who would later be incorporated into the church's congregation as well as its staff. Joseph F. Walker, a former slave who also published his own recollections, recalled the "parental upbringing" he experienced as a boy during the war years. In his memoirs, which were recorded by John J. Lanier, Walker described his own path to salvation, as well as the dramatic appointments that were exposed to him as an adult. He opened the piece with a brief history of his induction into the faith:

I was born December 17, 1854. My owners were the Goodwins. My original master was Col. William Goodwin who had two sets of children…The War Between the States had not begun then. My first recollection was the mustering at Spotsylvania Court House. My next recollection was when my master, Bert Goodwin, left to go to Aquia.

I went to live with Judge Barton in the Fall of 1873. I got there $10.00 per month and I joined the church in 1877. I remember now Mrs. Barton's gentle words. She came to me in the pantry and said: "Joseph, you are going to be baptized today?" I said: "Yes'm." She said: "Joseph don't stop there; your work has just begun." That is all she said, but those words live with me now.

I became Sexton of St. George's Church in 1878. I still continued to live with Judge Barton. My combined stipend as sexton of the Church and as Judge Barton's butler was $17.00 per month…My first religious impression was obtained from Mr. Cushionberry; from his having daily morning prayer. All the servants came to this service. I have kept it up ever since, and consider it one of the most valuable things I have derived from my Episcopalian friends.

Walker continued to serve at St. George's Church for years to come and also became a senior deacon at Shiloh Baptist Church (New Site). Over a period of forty-eight years, he served six rectors through their entire terms of service.

Like the neighboring denominations, St. George's Episcopal Church found itself caught in the middle of the "Great Divide" that left an indelible impression on the community. Even today, the interior walls of the church's steeple remain scarred by the shot and shell that rained down from Stafford Heights. Despite the rampant damage from the war years, St. George's continues to stand above the rubble as a beacon of hope, even in the most desperate of times.

Today

St. George's Episcopal Church remains as one of the largest congregations in all of Fredericksburg and it has become a favorite tourist attraction. Although extensive postwar rehabilitation required the patching of over twenty holes made by artillery rounds, the building resumed regular services as early as May of 1865. Since then the church has restored a spectacular forty-six-set pipe organ and installed several priceless Tiffany stained-glass windows. A major attraction at St. George's is the colonial-era cemetery that fills the adjacent courtyard. In 1951, church member Carrol H. Quenzel published a directory of the gravesites titled *Burials in St. George's Graveyard*. Her book used the inscriptions and notes that were copied by George H.S. King in 1940. Among the noteworthy graves that can be visited today are John Jones (buried in 1752), Anthony and Virginia Patton (relatives of General George S. Patton) and John Coalter (former owner of Chatham Manor).

FREDERICKSBURG PRESBYTERIAN CHURCH

Yesterday Dr. Brown preached in the Presbyterian Church; he prayed for "those who have been in authority over us and are now suffering, that the Lord might bless and comfort them," for "...the Lord might change their hearts, and make them enact wise and righteous laws," and that "God might deliver us from the curse of wicked rulers."

—journal of Lizzie Maxwell Alsop of Fredericksburg

Background

Located at 810 Princess Anne Street, the present Greek Revival–style structure was erected in 1833 and is the second oldest church in town. Due to Federal occupation during the War Between the States, the church was severely damaged inside and out. In support of the war effort, the church bell was given to the Confederacy to be melted down for cannons. During that time (1862), the building was also used as a Federal hospital, and Clara Barton, founder of the American Red Cross, attended to some of the twenty-six thousand or so wounded soldiers who were treated there from the Battles of Fredericksburg, the Wilderness and Spotsylvania Court House. After the war, the church bell was replaced (in 1870), the interior was restored and the congregation was reunited. Today the sanctuary still bears the scars of the shelling of Fredericksburg, when two cannonballs were embedded in one of its pilasters.

Church Origin

The Presbyterian Church is the second oldest church to have a presence in Virginia, preceded only by the Church of England itself. Following the settling of the Jamestown Colony by the Virginia Company in 1607, a proclamation was sent forth by King James's charter that "the word and services of God be preached, planted, and used according to the rites and doctrines of the Church of England." In the previous chapter, the resulting establishment of St. George's Episcopal Church was presented. The founding of the Virginia Presbyterian movement was in direct response to this.

Fredericksburg Presbyterian Church. *Courtesy Dawn S. Bowen, PhD.*

According to Dr. Edward Alvery Jr., author of *History of the Presbyterian Church of Fredericksburg 1808–1976*, the long and tedious separation from the Church of England to the Protestant-Presbyterian Reformation was a forced resolution based on differing theological views. He wrote:

> *The* [Virginia] *Company was controlled by Puritans, who at this time constituted a party within the Church of England opposed to the Prayer Book and inclined, most of them, toward Presbyterianism. The ministers they sent to the colony before 1624, notably Alexander Whitaker and George Keith, organized their churches informally on the Presbyterian plan…Scotch Presbyterians had come from tidewater Virginia early in the seventeenth century. However, no attempt was made to organize distinctly Presbyterian congregations until, late in the century, Francis Makemie and Josiah Mackie organized congregations recognized as such by the laws of the colony.*

Therefore, Francis Makemie is considered by most to be the founder of Presbyterianism in America. He was directly responsible for the establishment of many of the region's earliest churches, as well as its tenets, and the forming of the Presbytery of Philadelphia, the first of its kind in America. Over the next century, the Presbyterian movement grew at a rapid pace, as Virginia's citizens became disenchanted with the Church of England and, in some cases, dissatisfied with the state of the Episcopal Church.

In 1806, the Reverend Samuel Blaine Wilson started a small ministry in Fredericksburg after preaching at the courthouse on the first Sunday of January. At the time, he found the role of religion to be particularly lacking in the day-to-day lives of the town's citizens. He noted that few attended the Episcopal church and that there were "pious people" among the various denominations, but that their preachers in general were not necessarily the most educated of men. Wilson also added that he had found a mere three members of the Presbyterian Church.

With the assistance of his fellow brethren, especially an Irish gentleman named John Mark, Reverend Wilson was able to provide a service that satisfied the community's desire for a new spiritual option. He continued to preach in various public forums, which came to be known around town as "Wilson's Church." Many of the city's most prominent families were influenced by Wilson's enthusiasm for the Gospel. They quickly converted to the Presbyterian denomination and this, in turn, drew additional members from the current Episcopalian congregation. Many of these defectors never returned, and from 1806 to 1808, the Episcopal church had no "official" rector. The two ministers that served there during the next four years (until 1812) apparently did little to expand the church or rejuvenate its membership.

As the authority of the "King's church" continued to stagnate, a new and more capable rector, Dr. Edward C. McGuire, took over in 1813 and served there until 1858. In his memoirs, McGuire stated that, at the time of his arrival, there were "not more than 12 communicants." In retrospect, it is he who deserves credit for reinvigorating the Episcopal church and restoring the congregation to its original membership. Over the years, the balance was restored between all of the churches of Fredericksburg. As the population grew, so did the need for additional houses of worship. The Presbyterian church, in particular, was blessed with some of the most celebrated ministers in the history of the city.

The War

An exceptional gentleman named Reverend Beverly Tucker Lacy became one of the most influential ministers of the entire Civil War period. The son of Reverend William Sterling Lacy, Beverly was born in nearby Prince William County, Virginia, on February 21, 1819. He received his secondary education at Washington College, which was later renamed Washington and Lee University. He graduated with a bachelor's degree in 1843. Lacy attended the prestigious Princeton Theological Seminary and was licensed to preach in 1846. He obtained his master's degree in 1847 and held positions as a pastor in Winchester and Salem, Virginia, as well as Lexington, Kentucky, before returning to Fredericksburg. He served the Presbyterian church in 1862. In 1863, Reverend Lacy carried the mission of the church with him when he became a chaplain in the Second Corps of the Confederate Army of Northern Virginia under the command of General Thomas "Stonewall" Jackson.

After realizing a lack of participation in the early war effort by the church, General Jackson sent a letter to the Southern Presbyterian General Assembly, petitioning them for support. In it he stated:

Each branch of the Christian Church should send into the army some of its most prominent ministers who are distinguished for their piety, talents and zeal; and such ministers should labor to produce concert of action among chaplains and Christians in the Army. These ministers should give special attention to preaching to regiments which are without chaplains, and induce them to take steps to get chaplains, to let the regiments name the denominations from which they desire chaplains selected, and then to see that suitable chaplains are secured. A bad selection of a chaplain may prove a curse instead of a blessing.

Despite the lack of readily available clergymen in the early Confederate army, Jackson took the initiative in 1863 and appointed Reverend Beverly Tucker Lacy as a personal minister to his staff. Lacy's task was to maintain daily prayer rituals for the commander and his troops, whether in camp or on the march. Whenever possible, a strict schedule of morning and evening worship on the Sabbath, as well as Wednesday prayer meetings, was adhered to at all costs. Reverend Lacy routinely led the services, which were often attended by Major General Robert E. Lee and his officers.

As the courageous reputation of the "Stonewall Brigade" continued to grow, so did its pious commander's mission for spreading the Gospel. Reverend Lacy's energizing speeches quickly became popular events for saved and unsaved soldiers alike, who attended his sermons by the thousands. General Jackson later recalled one particular event that summarized the success of his chaplain's ministry. He wrote: "It was a noble sight to see there those, who led our armies to victory and upon whom the eyes of the nation are turned with admiration and gratitude, melted in tears at the story of the cross and the exhibition of the love of God to the repenting and return sinner."

It was the Reverend Lacy who buried the amputated arm of Jackson on his brother's property at Ellwood Plantation in Orange County. Long before the accidental wounding of his commander, it would be Reverend Lacy's own flock that would come under fire and occupation by Federal forces repeatedly during the War Between the States. The city of Fredericksburg changed hands several times over the course of the conflict, starting in April of 1862. Due to its strategic location, centered between the Union capital of Washington, D.C., and the Confederate capital of Richmond, as well as its proximity to fordable water and railroads, the town was regarded as a valuable piece of real estate by both sides.

The Presbyterian church was also considered an important asset by Northern and Southern Christians alike, particularly with regard to the spiritual nourishment required before marching off to war. A chaplain from South Carolina, writing from camp to the *Southern Presbyterian*, reported, "I am both astonished and I trust grateful to see how attentively officers and men listen to the preached word, and how eagerly they read the tracts which I have been able to supply."

A contemporary also recalled the religious enthusiasm that spread from the citizens throughout the ranks of the Confederate army. He wrote:

As some of the Confederate troops were marching through Fredericksburg, VA, with bristling bayonets and rumbling artillery, a fair lady appeared on the steps of a dark

Presbyterian church building. *Courtesy Fredericksburg Tourism*.

Jackson's arm marker at Ellwood. *Courtesy of the author*.

General Thomas "Stonewall" Jackson. *Courtesy Museum of Confederacy.*

brown mansion, her arms filled with Testaments, which with gracious kindness and gentle courtesy, she distributed to the passing soldiers. The eagerness with which they were received, the pressing throng, the earnest thanks, the unspoken blessings upon the giver…all made up a picture as beautiful as any that ever shone out amid the dark relatives of war.

It should be noted that the local Presbyterians, in particular, were very active in the distribution of testaments and other religious materials to the armies of Virginia. Prior to the outbreak of the Civil War, the American Bible Society, based in New York, handled the production and delivery of most Protestant-based materials, including Bibles and tracts. After the conflict began, an entirely new system had to be formed in order to meet the needs of the Southern congregations. Many of these dilemmas were addressed in the minutes of the Presbyterian Church's General Assembly. One major point addressed the need to establish a new chapter of the Bible Society to shoulder the task of producing and distributing religious materials in the Confederate states.

Another concern pertained to the issue of camp worship and the negative effect of military operations on the Sabbath. A letter was drafted and forwarded to Confederate President Jefferson Davis. It stated:

To the President of the Confederate States of America: Sir: The General Assembly of the Presbyterian Church in the Confederate States of America venture to address your Excellency in reference to the desecration of the Sabbath in our armies. In common with very many of our fellow-citizens, we have been deeply pained at the prevailing disregard of an institution which lies at the foundation, not only of Christianity, but of morality as well. The God who ordained the Sabbath is that God to whom we are accustomed to appeal for the justice of our cause—upon whom we are calling for that help which alone can avail to bring our country successfully and triumphantly through the present great struggle. How can we hope for God's blessing, or consistently ask it, when we are deliberately and habitually setting aside, and treating with contempt that which He has enjoined upon us to remember and keep holy?

By establishing the presence of chaplains in the camps and offering regular worship services, influential believers like General Thomas "Stonewall" Jackson were able to provide for their troops' spiritual needs. This ultimately aided the soldiers in dealing with the horrific recollections of war. Unfortunately, Fredericksburg's citizens would also experience a horrifying memory and a nightmare of epic proportions back on the homefront. In a letter first published in a December 1962 issue of *The Civil War Times*, Major Francis E. Pierce, a Federal officer, recalled the anarchy and vandalism that occurred shortly after the Battle of Fredericksburg. He wrote:

Troops crossing all day long. Fredericksburg given up to pillage and destruction. Boys came into our place loaded with silver pitchers, silver lamps and casters, etc. Great three-story houses furnished magnificently were broken into their contents scattered over the

City of churches skyline. *Courtesy U.S. National Park Service.*

floors and trampled on by the muddy feet of the soldiers. Splendid alabaster vases and pieces of statuary were thrown at 6 & 700 dollar mirrors…I can't even begin to describe the scenes of destruction. It was so throughout the city, and from its appearance very many wealthy families must have inhabited it.

Throughout the conflict, the town's citizens periodically entered into a day-to-day social existence with the United States Army that occupied the area. Often Secessionists and Unionists would find themselves worshiping at the same church service. A regular attendee of the Presbyterian church, Mrs. Jane Howison Beale meticulously recorded in her diary the effect of the army's presence over the course of the summer in 1862. She recalled that Federal troops had attended church in large numbers and that Reverend Lacy's sermons, in particular, were popular among the Northern soldiers. She added:

We had a crowded church today as there was no service in the Episcopal or Baptist churches and with parts of three congregations and more than a hundred Yankees our church was full. Mr. L. sometimes offends our tastes by rather more attention to the Yankees than we like to see paid, but preaches very good sermons to make up for it.

The Federal army eventually moved on and things in the town of Fredericksburg appeared to return to normal. That is, until the fateful day in December of 1862 when artillerists from both sides rained shell and shot down upon the city. To this day, ordnance still remains buried in the exterior of the church building. In the left column of the portico, there are cannonballs placed in indentations that were created by shells fired during the bombardment of the city from guns positioned near Falmouth. These balls were taken from a miscellaneous lot at Hunter's Foundry, where unused cannonballs were melted and used in casting farm implements after the war. They were donated to the church by Mr. P.V. Daniel, who was a manager at the foundry, and placed into the indentations in 1886 by the sexton, George Van Dueerson.

Following their disastrous charges toward the stone wall at Marye's Heights, the Union army commandeered the Presbyterian church for use as a field hospital. The official reports following the Battle of Fredericksburg state that the Union forces suffered approximately 12,653 casualties. The Confederate losses were much fewer, but were still considerable. Many of the wounded on both sides would die, not from their battlefield wounds, but from the disease and infections that would strike them after medical care and amputations were performed. The conditions at these churches, which were turned into makeshift medical sites, were far too often deplorable.

Union troops/teamsters at Fredericksburg. *Courtesy Library of Congress.*

One woman who was determined to improve the healthcare of wounded soldiers everywhere was Ms. Clara Barton, founder of the Red Cross and celebrated Civil War humanitarian. Following the engagement, Barton crossed the river on the same pontoon bridges the Federals had used. She wrote of the horrors that greeted her on the other side: "I had crossed over into that city of death, its roofs riddled by shells, its very church a crowded hospital, every street a battle line, every hill a rampart."

According to her own accounts, she rendered aid to the sick and dying in both the Episcopal and Presbyterian sanctuaries, although her presence at the Presbyterian chapel has been questioned due to a lack of outside sources. This debate is understandable, as Barton also wrote of being called from church to church, even stopping to administer aid to a severely wounded infantryman who turned out to be the sexton of her own childhood church in Worcester, Massachusetts. She returned across the river to the Lacy house at Chatham Manor, where she estimated there to be no fewer than twelve hundred wounded men crowded into the rooms of the mansion. Like her comrades in blue, Barton would return later in the war to the same town and churches to nurse troops felled in the bloody Battles of the Wilderness and Spotsylvania Court House. The traumatic events of these wartime trials remained ingrained in her memory and a biographer stated, "The memories of Fredericksburg remained with her distinct and terrible to the day of her death." As a testament to the goodwill and charity of Clara Barton, a bronze plaque was dedicated in the Presbyterian churchyard on September 25, 1962. It reads:

In Memory of
1862–1962
CLARA BARTON

Founder of the American Red Cross, a devoted
Nurse and tireless organizer who knew no enemy
but the unfeeling heart. We walk the ways she took
in easing the suffering at the Battle of Fredericksburg,
when the churches became military hospitals.

Erected by
Civil War Centennial Committee of Fredericksburg

Like all congregations, Fredericksburg Presbyterian also petitioned the United States government for compensation for damages incurred during the Battle of Fredericksburg, as well as Chancellorsville, the Wilderness and Spotsylvania Court House. As a result, it was also subjected to the same investigation and claims inquiry as its fellow churches. According to Court Claim No. 11793, the Presbyterian church of Fredericksburg petitioned for $3,500 in damages. Depositions were eventually taken in Fredericksburg on April 13, 1905, before E.F. Chesley, a notary public, and once again in the presence of G.W. Hott, counsel for the claimants, and W.W. Scott, attorney for the defendant.

Red Cross founder Clara Barton. *Courtesy Library of Congress.*

These transcripts presented eyewitness accounts of the damage that was done to the church by the occupying Union army. In his testimony, congregation and Sunday school member S.H. Beale recalled the destruction of the Presbyterian church during the Battles of Fredericksburg and Chancellorsville. He stated: "I know Federal forces occupied the building for a hospital. They tore all of the pews out of the church; the pulpit was so badly damaged it had to be taken out after the war and repaired, the church was completely gutted…The Federal forces used most of the pews to mark the graves of the soldiers." A relative, Robert C. Beale, recalled that the walls had been "badly damaged by cannon fire" and that the windows were all "smashed to pieces." All present testified to the deadly and destructive artillery bombardment that preceded the battle.

In addition to its use for religious revivals by the defending Confederate forces, the Presbyterian church also served wounded Rebels, sometimes after they had been taken as prisoners. Wilbur Wightman Gramling of the Fifth Florida Infantry Regiment wrote of his experiences as a wounded prisoner of war in a diary he kept after falling into enemy hands. From May 6 to May 14 of 1864, following his participation in the Wilderness Campaign, he recorded his experiences. He wrote:

Arrived in Fredericksburg only this morning. Established hospital in a Presbyterian Church. Nothing to eat but hard bread, coffee, beef tea, and every two or three days ½ oz. boiled beef…The church is still my place of rendezvous. Diet remains the same. Rolls, ham & preserves for breakfast….Nothing new today. Wounded are still coming in in considerable numbers.

Perhaps one of the most vivid descriptions came from Thomas Walker Gilmer, who recalled:

The terrible fighting at the Wilderness and Spotsylvania Court House brought thousands of Federal wounded to the place. They were removed through precaution as rapidly as possible, only to make room, however, for new scenes of horror, as fresh loads of mangled, bleeding men were brought in from day to day. At one time there were 20,000 badly wounded men in town. At no time during these battles were there many less. Every house was a hospital, with but very few exceptions, and the families, narrowed down to the smallest space, were to hear the cries of the sufferers day and night, and be subjected to all the awful sights of a military hospital. The churches were occupied; and the ruin commenced by the shelling, was now completed. From all but one church the pews were removed, with all the other furniture. These pews and carpets, etc. were destroyed. This work nearly completed the desolation of the town.

For the most part, the enlisted soldiers frequented Fredericksburg Presbyterian Church. But it was also visited by some of the Confederacy's top commanders, including General Thomas "Stonewall" Jackson. Ironically, one of the general's most trusted aides, Captain James P. Smith, later became a pastor at the church. Smith was also the officer who assisted Jackson after he was accidentally shot three times by his own troops following the first day of the Battle of Chancellorsville. Years later, Smith remembered his experiences in Fredericksburg with his beloved superior. He wrote of one trip in November of 1862, when he accompanied Jackson into town for a strategy planning session to prepare for an imminent Federal attack. He recalled, "Although it was Sunday morning, no church bells were ringing, and the streets were almost deserted, as were the homes. A few soldiers were in the streets. We sat in our saddles at the corner of the bank and the churches."

In a letter written to the *Daily Star*, Mrs. Vivian Minor Fleming of the Kenmore Association related Dr. Smith's memory of the incident. She wrote:

Dismounting from his horse on the corner of George and Princess Anne Streets, near the Presbyterian Church, he [General Jackson] stood for a long time plunged in deep thought. Captain Smith, tired of waiting, asked permission to go and water his horse at the river. The general [Jackson] replied, "Better not, Captain, some of those people might get you." But Dr. Smith said he did go and when he returned he found some of the gentlemen of the town, attracted by the stars on the general's uniform (he had recently acquired a handsome new uniform) talking to him.

On month later, following the bombardment and the ensuing battle at Fredericksburg, Smith recorded that General Jackson was "deeply concerned about the suffering population of Fredericksburg." He added that his commander had "issued an appeal to the officers and men of his command for their relief, and $30,000 passed through my [Smith's] hands, the receipts from which the mayor of the town are in the library at Fredericksburg."

In recognition of the charitable providence of the Christian general and honoring his presence, a special tablet marking Jackson's visit was formally presented to the Presbyterian church in 1924 by Miss Francis Thompson, president of the Fredericksburg Chapter of the United Daughters of the Confederacy, and accepted by the trustees and officers of the church. The marble marker is located in the corner of the churchyard and bears an inscription that reads, "Gen. Stonewall Jackson, by Gen. Lee's request, on this corner, planned the Battle of Fredericksburg. November 27, 1862. U.D.C."

Reconstruction

Following the end of the war years, many of the town's citizens, both black and white, returned to devastated businesses, churches and homes. Fredericksburg and the surrounding area were left in ruins. The town was a shell of its former self. The people soon realized a need to find a suitable place to bury and honor their dead. The Presbyterian church took the initiative in this endeavor and called a special meeting to determine how to properly honor the Confederate casualties who had been haphazardly buried around the outskirts of the town and on the adjacent battlefields. It was determined that two cemeteries would be required and that Fredericksburg and Spotsylvania would have separate grounds.

It was also determined at the meeting that the women of the city would form a Ladies Memorial Association, the first chartered in the South, to raise money for the establishment of a formal Fredericksburg Confederate Cemetery. On May 10, 1865, one month after the surrender of the Army of Northern Virginia at Appomattox Court House, this group of remarkable ladies held its first meeting in the basement of the Presbyterian church, as the rest of the building was in ruins. The members began to establish fundraising initiatives. Shortly thereafter, the church treasury began to fill with money secured from donations and charitable events. Former Confederate officer and Presbyterian member Major James Horace Lacy was appointed to represent the association. He began to travel on a fundraising mission and secured generous donations from Shreveport, New Orleans, Baltimore and even New York. In Louisiana, the major is rumored to have addressed what his peers would have called an audience of "carpetbaggers," who were apparently so moved by his oration that they collectively voted to contribute $5,000 for the cause.

After acquiring sufficient funds, a site was selected adjoining the existing cemetery in the western part of the city. Next, the unpleasant task of retrieving those who had been buried in fields across the area, often in haste, was undertaken. In the end, a total of 3,353 bodies were exhumed and transported from the surrounding battlefields to the new cemetery, where each one was reinterred according to his state. This kept comrades together and reinforced the feeling of a band of brothers who had fought and fallen together. As with all local Civil War burial sites, a sentinel was required to watch over the dead. Years later, additional funds were gathered for a granite monument featuring a lone Confederate sentry. The marker was dedicated on Memorial Day in June of 1884 and featured an inscription that read, "To the Confederate Dead." Several members of the Presbyterian church were at the forefront of the statue project. They included Mrs. J.H. Lacy, Miss Ann Carter, Doctor F.P. Wellford and an Episcopalian brother named John Wallace.

Another apparent mission of the Presbyterian church at the end of the war was the need to reestablish and reinvigorate the congregation. In September of 1865, there were only 60 members, a remnant of the 175 regular communicants who had filled the rolls in 1861. The building itself was barely usable. Part of the roof had collapsed and the pews had been torn out and used as makeshift coffins for Confederate officers. The carpets and furnishings had been stolen or destroyed and the floors and walls were covered in blood, mud and filth.

Thomas Walker Gilmer, a graduate of Thomas Jefferson's University of Virginia, was a lawyer who had answered "the call" and left the courtroom for the seminary. After completing his studies at the Union Theological Seminary of Virginia in Richmond, he enlisted in the Confederate army and served as a chaplain in Lee's Army of Northern Virginia. At the end of the war, Gilmer came to Fredericksburg and was officially named pastor of the Presbyterian church in June of 1866. That December, he wrote in his diary about how his new flock had set about to start the rebuilding process. He recalled:

With cheerful, Christian hope, they fitted up the basement of their church, organized a prayer meeting, invited a minister to labor with them, trusting to the Lord to make provision for him as well as themselves. The remnants of the scattered and broken flock united their prayers and their efforts. Two services on Sabbath and one in the week were instituted, and the Sabbath-school re-commenced. Now more flourishing than it ever was, numbering seventy-eight scholars, with a full corps of teachers. The minister is amply supplied with all he could wish. But more than this; through the kind and generous sympathy of God's people, they feel encouraged to hope that during the next spring they will worship in their church.

Under Gilmer's tutelage, the Presbyterian congregation grew rapidly. By the end of 1866, there were 134 communicants and 150 children who were active, participating members. By the following fall, there were over 300 members and students attending regular Sunday school programs. Unfortunately, the reverend would fall victim to a fatal heart attack in April of 1869. It was reported in the church minutes that his last words were, "My Redeemer!"

One of the most famous and endearing stories surrounding Fredericksburg Presbyterian Church is the story of its bells. When the first sanctuary was erected in town in 1833, a beautiful bell was installed in the belfry overlooking the corner of Charles and Amelia Streets. It continued to announce services for many years, until the "call to arms" that followed Virginia's secession. Answering the need for sacrifice, the bell was donated to the Confederacy so that it could be melted down and used for the manufacture of cannons. For nearly a decade, the belfry at Fredericksburg Presbyterian Church remained empty. The women of the congregation once again stepped forward and raised over $800 to cover the cost of a replacement bell. Cast by the Baltimore company of Joshua Register and Son, a 1,884-pound bell was acquired and installed in September of 1870. A raised inscription on the bell reads, "Blessed is the people who know the joyful sound—Psalm LXXXIX–XV." On the other side it states, "Purchased by the Ladies of Fredericksburg 1870 to replace the bell freely given in 1862 to the Confederate States and molten into cannon, our land, our laws, our altars to defend."

In an unidentifiable newspaper clipping on file at the Fredericksburg/Spotsylvania National Military Park, a soldier named William Nick who served with the Rockbridge Artillery recalled the events surrounding the celebratory atmosphere following the new bell's installation. The reporter quoting Nick wrote:

> The Manassas Democrat *calls attention to the bell in the Presbyterian Church at Fredericksburg saying that it "has a history of which many people should be proud." The placing of this bell in the steeple in 1870 had a direct connection with the War for Southern Independence. Workmen were lately repairing the church and in so doing their attention was attracted to the inscription on the bell: "Blessed is the people that know the joyful sound."…Some day some one will write an interesting book about the many historic bells in this country, and, when it is written, this old bell of Fredericksburg will be included, which has ever been characteristic of the women of Fredericksburg.*

As the 1880s approached, the Presbyterian church began to broaden its scope of ministry to other groups not reflected in the current congregation. Missions and ministries abroad became successful ventures as foreign relations and spreading the Good News of the Gospel became a prime directive. However, according to church minutes taken in April of 1880, newly freed blacks were not included in their evangelism. The session stated, "Nothing has been done for the coloured people by our church; though it is a matter now held in consideration." One year later, the annual year-end summary stated, "We are not yet able to report any work for the Coloured People in our midst, though we have long desired to find an open door." Finally in 1882, a "Coloured Sunday School" was started, although it would later be suspended and then disbanded all together. By 1884, it was recorded, "No effort made this year to maintain a [Sunday] School for The Coloured People."

In the years following the South's surrender and subsequent reconstruction, perhaps no one wrote more on the role of religion in the Confederacy, and the experiences of notable figures in places such as Fredericksburg, than Dr. James P. Smith. After serving in the field and at the pulpit, Smith published several books, including *A King and a Father*, *Religious Character of Stonewall Jackson*, *Jackson at Chancellorsville*, *Brightside Idyls* and *Lee at*

Gettysburg, as well as an address delivered at the Virginia Military Institute (VMI). The last surviving member of Jackson's staff, he was also a certified evangelist and an editor of the *Central Presbyterian*.

In 1891, his congregation heralded him in the highest regard upon his retirement. One paper that was written for the occasion stated, "As a pastor and a friend, his sympathy and love for his people…have been conspicuous and constant…A pastoral relation of twenty-one years, marked by such fidelity, efficiency and fruitfulness, cannot be severed without a painful stress of feeling…and a sorrowful sense of loss."

Today

The Presbyterian church remains one of the largest congregations in the city of Fredericksburg, as well as one of the most visited landmarks in the downtown area. Focused on the educational aspects of faith, it provides opportunities for all children, youth and adults to continue the development of their faith through worship, education and missions. Some of these opportunities are presented through Sunday school, Vacation Bible School, Presbyterian Women's Circle, Men's Group, Women's Bible Study, Youth Group, confirmation, Wednesday Night Supper and Activities, retreat, mission projects and workshops.

FREDERICKSBURG UNITED METHODIST CHURCH

The bandage with which my own wound was bound up was part of a white skirt belonging to an elderly woman...Seeing the need of a bandage she loosed her skirt, cut it into strips, and handed them to my father, who proceeded to dress my own and other soldiers' wounds.
—*wounded Union soldier carried to the Methodist church in Fredericksburg*

Background

The United Methodist church was established in Fredericksburg in 1802 and was originally located on George Street. According to its own declaration, "Methodism in Fredericksburg was formally constituted in April, 1802 as a station in the Baltimore Conference. After a rocky start, it began to grow in the 1820's when John Kobler, a retired Methodist minister, and his wife, Mary, became members. Inspired by the lay leadership of Kobler, the church outgrew its small frame building, and in 1842, built a new brick edifice on Hanover Street at the location it occupies today." Unfortunately, this church was destroyed during the Civil War in 1862. It was rebuilt in 1882 as the Fredericksburg Methodist Episcopal Church.

Church Origin

Perhaps no other church in this study was so stirred by the debate over the institution of slavery as the Methodist church. In fact, opposing views over the African slave trade turned members against one another, resulting in a separation of the congregation. To fully understand the effect of this forced division, in lieu of resolution, one must understand the stubbornness and resolve that was founded in the roots of the Methodist movement back in England.

In May of 1738, a young clergyman from London named John Wesley experienced what many believers refer to as a "religious awakening." Distraught with the questionable political practices of the Anglican community, Wesley believed that it had lost touch with its holy obligations in favor of the pursuit of power. In his eyes, the Church of

Fredericksburg United Methodist Church. *Courtesy Dawn S. Bowen, PhD.*

England, in particular, had become abusive and was out of touch with the population. The corruption of the monarchy in years past had also blemished the reputation and trustworthiness of the institution. Wesley's dramatic epiphany came at a time when social and economic changes were everywhere, as his country struggled to evolve from a pastoral economy to a modern industrialized nation. As a result, the very notion of a state-controlled church came under scrutiny, as Christians and skeptics alike began to seek other forms of enlightenment. It was the dawning of a new age of learning, when everyday people strived to achieve a higher level of social and spiritual intelligence.

John Wesley may not have been fully aware of the scope of his vision, but he was steadfast in the pursuit of it. John Janey Johnson's bicentennial book, titled *John Kobler's Dream: A History of the Fredericksburg United Methodist Church 1802–1975*, stated the following regarding Wesley:

> He was keenly aware of the fact that he had just had a joyful Christian experience which he wanted very much to share with the people of England. He began to preach, being ably assisted by his brother, Charles, and George Whitefield, both of whom had been active with him as members of a small group of serious thinkers at Oxford which had been nicknamed "Methodists" because of the methodical attention to the ordinances of the Church. Their enthusiasm and fiery evangelism had a disturbing effect on the

existing congregations and most rectors and their parishioners recoiled with distaste at the preaching of these "enthusiasts" so that all pulpits were soon closed to them.

This blackballing resulted in the evolution of alternative worshiping venues. Secret "Methodist Societies" began forming all over the British Isles. Wesley and his rapidly expanding flock of followers were not discouraged, and their movement became a popular option for religious citizens who had become disenchanted with their faith due to the rapid moral deterioration of the government-run institutions. They also appreciated the philosophy that instilled the concept that it was possible for commoners to have a personal relationship with their Savior. This foundation of "bringing people to the altar" instead of distancing them ultimately helped to ignite the entire Protestant movement, which took a different philosophy from that of the Roman Catholic and Anglican Churches. Inevitably, as with all Protestant beliefs, Methodism spread overseas to America, where colonists were exploring the New World and seeking refuge to practice a religious freedom that was not readily accepted in their homeland.

Although initially interrupted by the Revolutionary War, the denomination was eventually established at a revival event recorded as the "Christmas conference of 1784," which was held at the Lovely Lane Chapel in Baltimore, Maryland. The result was the official christening of the Methodist Episcopal Church of America. Almost immediately upon its formation, the ordained superintendents of Methodism began an intensive campaign to spread their new theology across the land.

At once, a controversy erupted, as the antislavery views of some of the church's first preachers did not sit well with many Southern citizens. One gentleman in particular, Dr. Thomas Coke, was mobbed many times during his travels for preaching against the institution of slavery. Additionally, many Christians, who were either slaveholders themselves or supported the practice, refused to attend any services offered by the good doctor. This divide over racial equality separated the church and slowed its initial establishment in Virginia.

In March of 1802, a major milestone in the Methodist Church occurred in the little town of Fredericksburg. That was the year that one of the most active Methodist ministers of the time, Bishop Francis Asbury, journeyed to the city and preached his first public sermon. The title of his address was "Seek Ye the Lord While He May Be Found." Shortly afterward, the town was added as a "Methodist station" and was placed into the Alexandria District of the Baltimore Annual Conference. Mr. John Pitts was appointed the pastor in charge and Mr. Daniel Hitt was named as the presiding elder.

From here on, it is difficult to pinpoint the exact details as to the official chartering of the first Methodist Episcopal church in town. The lack of records makes it difficult to explain the sudden establishment of the congregation. However, it is recorded that the initial congregation grew steadily and, within months, numbered seventy-three members.

Even Bishop Asbury was surprised by the rapid increase of his flock and he made a point of commenting on it in his journal. He wrote, "Glory, Glory, be to God." He later credited his own church for inspiring other young Protestant faiths to follow in its

Confederate Cavalry General
J.E.B. Stuart. *Courtesy Museum of
Confederacy*.

footsteps. In 1810 he wrote, "The Methodists have done great good here; since they began to preach, the Baptists and the Presbyterians have built meeting houses."

Unfortunately for the Methodists, the unity exhibited by their new neighbors did not continue to prosper in their own sanctuary. Just a few decades into its existence, the issue of slavery ignited a feud within the congregation itself. The results were drastic to say the least. D.M. Conway published an essay titled "Fredericksburg First and Last" in the June 1887 issue of the *Magazine of American History* (vol. 17, no. 6) that explained the results of the conflict:

> *While Young Virginia was hastening to the new standard, Old Virginia never tired of its conservatism. But events conspired to make Fredericksburg an especial battle-field of the contending principles. The division of the Methodist Episcopal Church (1844), caused by the suspension of a slave-holding bishop (Andrews), brought conflict into the large congregation at Fredericksburg. The town was on the border between the Virginia and Baltimore Conferences, while belonging to the latter. The antislavery traditions of Methodism had been once strong enough to suspend from his local ministry the founder of the society, Rev. John Kobler, because he had married a wife (the widow Early) who*

refused to part with her slaves. The old Wesleyan testimony now held at Fredericksburg its southmost stronghold, which was defended by powerful preachers (notably the Rev. Norval Wilson) against eloquent champions of the pro-slavery principle, of whom was Rev. Dr. William Smith, sometime President of Randolph Macon College. The pro-slavery elements at length seceded and built a church of their own; and, indeed, it was not until 1865 that the two societies were finally consolidated under the Methodist Church South.

Still, the arguments over slavery in the Old Dominion had been a long-standing debate for almost one hundred years before the Methodists split over it. According to an article printed in an 1887 issue of *American History Magazine*, "In 1790, Virginia claimed 293,427 registered slaves, which was more than seven times the number in the Northern states combined." Ironically, it also stated that the Reverend Morgan Godwin of the early English Church was reported to be one of the first clergymen "who ever lifted up his voice against the African slave trade."

This sentiment most likely came as a great surprise, due to the fact that the proslavery sentiment of many transplanted Englishmen prevented the freeing of Negroes upon the victory of independence. Emancipation continued to be a hotly contested topic among Christians for decades and Virginia remained in the center of the controversy. Many antislavery proponents in Fredericksburg were drawn into a moral dilemma following secession over protecting their land or defending slavery.

The War

Prior to the Civil War, the building housing the Methodist Episcopal church stood as a charming, two-story brick structure located on the south side of Hanover Street, between Prince Edward and Princess Anne Streets. The congregation consisted of approximately 115 white members and 53 black members. In 1848, a large portion of the membership began an exodus, due to the acrimonious debate over slavery. In 1852 they constructed their own meetinghouse (Methodist Episcopal Church South), which was located one block from the parent church. In 1861, the original church rolls listed 164 members, while the new branch boasted 290 followers. Both sites would see significant action during the War Between the States and provide a gruesome service for the occupying Federal forces.

Despite their differences over slavery and secession, many Methodists from both churches would answer the "call to arms" in support of the newly declared Confederate States of America. A Sunday school superintendent in the Methodist Episcopal Church South, named Joseph W. Sener, served as a captain in a local company of militia called the Washington Guards who were later folded into the Thirteenth Regiment of General George Pickett's famous division. Sener had accompanied Colonel Robert E. Lee to Harpers Ferry in 1859 to deal with an uprising by abolitionist John Brown and was approaching his fifties at the time of the Civil War.

One extraordinary example of fulfilling one's duty is the story of a courageous woman who faithfully followed her husband into the field. Mrs. Lucy Ann Cox, the daughter of the *Weekly Advertiser*'s editor Jesse White, accompanied the Confederate forces under which her husband served for all four years of the war. Sharing in every peril and hardship, she assisted in cooking and washing for the troops and often ministered to the sick and wounded.

Robert Hodges's commemorative biography on the heroine, which was written for the Order of Southern Gray and titled *Lucy Ann Cox Chapter #4 Fredericksburg, Virginia*, stated:

> She accompanied the regiment to Manassas to join General Beauregard's army, enduring without a murmur the fatigue and privations of the long and wearisome march there and back to Aquia Creek. In March 1862 they were ordered to North Carolina, and from that date to the close of the war she was in the field—in every campaign, on every march—ever at her husband's side to minister to him when sick, to comfort him when dispirited.
>
> Her devotion won the praise and highest admiration from every rugged soldier and she became known by the sobriquet "PAWNEE" throughout Pickett's Division, but it was the members of Co. A that she fed when they were hungry; sheltered when they were exposed; and patched and washed for them when there was no one else. When the war was over, and the Cox's returned to Fredericksburg, the soldiers of Maury Camp of Confederate Veterans elected her by acclamation as honorary member of the camp and presented her with a Camp Badge. She wore the badge prominently and proudly at all reunions and on Memorial Day.
>
> Though Lucy became a victim of dropsy and found it exceedingly difficult to get about, she was in attendance at the reunion of Co. A at Alum Spring in August 1885, when J.K. Graeme, a photographer, was present and photographed the company. She participated at the table where the solids and sweetmeats were spread and enjoyed observing the music, dancing, croquet, swinging, target shooting and most of all, participating the relating of stories of the "tented field."
>
> She was also present at the reunion at Alum Spring in September 1886. The day was pleasant enough until time for the parties to return to their respective homes. Capt. John K. Anderson had obtained a wagon and with considerable help, managed to get the overly large Lucy on one edge of the seat. The road being an unused one and badly washed by recent freshets, and the weight being unevenly distributed, the wagon upset and spilled out the occupant, who, for a time, caused quite a racket. She was collected with whole bones, but the wagon was more or less demolished.
>
> The reporter had hoped to have a pleasant interview with the lady, but her indignant looks forbid he should venture into her presence until the next reunion when he would be surrounded by comrades. Lucy Ann Cox died on December 17, 1891, aged sixty-four, and was buried in the Fredericksburg Confederate Cemetery. Prof. Bowering's twenty-piece military band, in full uniform, provided the measured tread from the Methodist church to the cemetery, playing the funeral march. After a short religious service, the band played a sweetly solemn dirge.

Above left: Methodist Episcopal Church (North). Courtesy James Monroe Museum.

Above right: Methodist Episcopal Church (South). Courtesy James Monroe Museum.

Following her death, several friends erected a stone marker over her grave that read:

> *Lucy Ann Cox, wife of James A. Cox, died December 17, 1891, aged 64 years. A sharer of the toil, dangers, and privations of the 30th Va. Regiment Infantry, C.S.A., from 1861 to 1865, and died beloved and respected by the veterans of that command.*

In the spring of 1863, the Methodist church served as a house of worship for Confederate forces that were stationed in the downtown area. As was occurring across much of the South, a great revival had swept up Barksdale's famous Mississippi Brigade. The resulting meetings began in the Presbyterian church and then shifted to the larger Methodist Episcopal church, before moving to the Methodist Episcopal Church South and finally to the largest sanctuary in town, St. George's. The blend of denominations was an inspiration to all who participated. The participating clergy were also moved by the show of unity. Reverend W.J. Hoge recalled a particular service when he wrote, "We had a Presbyterian sermon, introduced by Baptists services, under the direction of a Methodist chaplain, in an Episcopal Church. Was not that a beautiful solution to the vexed problem of Christian union?"

It would be a very different setting one year later, when both buildings were commandeered for use as field hospitals in May of 1864. The main branch housed wounded soldiers for one regiment of the Union Second Corps, First Division. Simultaneously, the "South" branch held troops from the Ninth Corps, First Division and Fifth Corps, First Division. By May 21, the sanctuary hosted over 150 casualties. A nurse described the scene as follows:

Dr. Detmold and Dr. Vanderpool, two eminent surgeons of New York…were paralyzed by what they saw [in Fredericksburg]…*our wounded lay in pools of water…The next morning these two surgeons came to me and said: "If we open another church under better conditions than these, will you accompany us?" and I said "Yes." After they got their nerve*[,] *their splendid executive ability asserted itself and they had the pews knocked to pieces; under the backs and seats* [they] *put a cleat and made little beds to raise the wounded from the floor…day by day things are improving. An amputating table is improvised* [sic] *under a tree in the yard where these good men work indefatigably.*

Some local civilians volunteered to assist in the aid of the wounded, regardless of the color of their uniforms. Several senior ladies of Fredericksburg rallied together to provide charity and compassion to those in need—even if they were "the enemy." A young soldier recalled an angel of mercy of his own when he wrote:

For the first few days at Fredericksburg it was almost impossible to obtain bandages. The women, with a few exceptions, were bitter rebels and would do all they could to prevent us from finding or buying a single piece of cloth. The bandage with which my own wound was bound up was part of the white skirt belonging to an elderly lady who brought roses into the Southern Methodist Episcopal Church where I was lying, a Mrs. McCabe. Seeing the need of a bandage, she loosed her skirt, cut it into strips, and handed it to my father, who proceeded to dress my own and other soldier's wounds.

Throughout the Civil War, hundreds and sometimes even thousands of men would be left behind following a major engagement. Unfortunately, the evacuation of the wounded was a dreadfully primitive and difficult process. Casualties were separated using a triage procedure, whereby all the wounded that could travel were loaded into mile-long caravans of army wagons, some of which were designated as ambulances. Those who were too seriously injured to be moved, or were near death, would be left behind in field hospitals that were usually established in whatever large buildings were available. Members of the medical corps, as well as Christian organizations or the United States Sanitary Commission and sometimes local residents, would then be charged with caring for those left behind. So, in the event of a retreat, the fallen soldiers would inevitably be left to the care and compassion of the enemy.

Due to its relative proximity to the United States capital, Fredericksburg's Federal wounded were continuously being evacuated back across the Rappahannock River and north toward the U.S. Army hospitals in Washington, D.C. Many men were lined up in rows outdoors and prepped for transportation via water routes. The city's churches, farms and even estates such as Chatham Manor were filled to an overflowing capacity with the dead and dying.

Confederate cavalry commander J.E.B. Stuart commented on the brutal destruction of the Union army and subsequent suffering of the local civilian population. In a letter he penned to Custis Lee he wrote:

The victory won by us here is one of the neatest and cheapest of the war. Englishmen here who surveyed Solferino & all the battlefields of Italy say that the pile of dead on the plains of Fredericksburg exceeds anything of the sort ever seen by them…Fredericksburg is in ruins. It is the saddest sight I ever saw.

One of the officers assigned to the evacuation of his fallen comrades was Captain Anderson, who was the cousin of the "Angel of the Battlefield" and founder of the American Red Cross, Ms. Clara Barton. The soldier recalled the healthcare crisis that surrounded him as he struggled to carry out his hopeless mission. Offering the counter perspective to Stuart's letter, he later wrote:

Here every church in the city was a hospital and every one was full, while all around outside lay wounded men ready to take the places of those who were dying within or being removed to Washington, Alexandria and Baltimore, via Belle Plain. Every public building was full, while in the smaller houses were wounded men who had personal friends or relatives in the Christian or Sanitary Commission, or friends who had been passed from Washington for that purpose, and were being kindly cared for. The large agricultural warehouses were also full of soldiers, placed in rows, upon muddy and bloody blankets, while nurses were going up and down between the rows with pails of ice water.

Another soldier named Gerrish of the Twentieth Maine made two visits to Fredericksburg, one after being wounded near the Wilderness. In his personal memoirs, titled *Reminiscences of the War*, he recalled his own evacuation and the spiritual comfort that he received upon arrival at the Methodist church. He wrote:

The baggage wagon, drawn by six mules, in which twelve of us had been carried from the wilderness, halted by a little churchyard, where we were unloaded, and placed under the shade of some great trees. Slowly the wounded were taken from the carriages. By scores, hundreds and thousands they came. The church, the yard, every square, and many of the buildings, were filled with the suffering soldiers. Scores had died by the way and hundreds site the city of Fredericksburgh.

[A year later:] I reached the little churchyard. It was not filled with suffering humanity as it had been just one year before. A few worshipers had entered the sanctuary; a sweet song of prayer was rolling out so softly on the still, evening air; I listened, the words were so familiar:

> *"Jesus lover of my soul,*
> *Let me to thy bosom fly,*
> *When the nearer waters roll,*
> *While the tempests still are high."*

Sadly, thousands of the fallen soldiers never made it across the river or out of the city alive. Today, the nearby Fredericksburg National Cemetery testifies to the boys in blue

U.S. Court of Claims document. *Courtesy U.S. National Park Service.*

who passed away either on the field or in the church sanctuaries where they awaited medical attention. It is the final resting place for over fifteen thousand United States soldiers. The Federal troops that are buried there include those who died of illness in the camps and in the four major battles around Fredericksburg, as well the Mine Run and North Anna Campaigns. Only about 20 percent of the soldiers are identified. Confederates who died in the Fredericksburg area were interred in Confederate cemeteries in Fredericksburg and Spotsylvania.

Reconstruction

Like all of the neighboring congregations, Fredericksburg Methodist Episcopal Church and its sister parish at Fredericksburg Methodist Episcopal Church South emerged from the Civil War battered, scarred and traumatized. Both the buildings and believers were damaged physically, mentally and spiritually. In 1865, Reverend John Lanahan petitioned a claim from the U.S. government on behalf of Fredericksburg Methodist Church for damages amounting to $1,087.40. This was a relatively small sum compared to requests from other churches, yet the claim was returned "disallowed." Years later, it would be reviewed, investigated and validated.

As the rest of the nation was in the process of reuniting and seeking forgiveness and reconciliation, so too was the Methodist faith, which had been torn apart over the institution of slavery, much like the rest of the country. The end of the War Between the

States meant more than just the conclusion of physical fighting. It also marked the end of political and social division. Following the South's surrender, the Baltimore Conference voted to become part of the Methodist Episcopal Church South, thus opening the door for a unification of the two split congregations.

Eventually the George Street branch was absorbed into the Hanover Street Church, and the Methodist family of Fredericksburg was finally together again. The reunited church of over two hundred members became part of the Washington District and the Baltimore Conference. Members returned to worship together at the George Street sanctuary and leased the Hanover site to a branch of Episcopalians who had left St. George's in order to form the Trinity Episcopal Church.

Of all the churches that filed grievances against the Federal government in the early 1900s, none appeared more thorough, or had more witness testimonies, than the trustees of the Fredericksburg Methodist Episcopal Church South. Their lengthy and detailed petition to the Court of Claims (No. 11,616 Cong.) was now for $3,000. Their opening argument stated:

> *To the Honorable the Court of Claims:*
>
> *Your undersigned petitioners, P.V.D. Conway, J.T. Lowery, and George A. Walker, trustees of the Methodist Episcopal Church South, of Fredericksburg, Virginia respectfully represent:*
>
> *That during the late civil war, and on or about December 15, 1862, the military forces of the United States under command of General Burnside, used, occupied and damaged the church building of the Methodist Episcopal Church South of Fredericksburg, Virginia. That at the time the building was finally abandoned by the said military forces all of the pews, furniture, fixtures and interior were destroyed, and the walls and roof badly damaged. That the cost to restore the building to the condition in which it was at the time the said military forces first used and damaged the same, was the sum of $3,000.00, for which no payment has been made.*

Unlike their contemporaries, who were all eventually granted a kindly gestured "political pardon" following each claims investigation, the Methodists took the initiative by boldly stating their loyalty to the Union in the opening statement. This was probably due to their antislavery stance, which caused the separation of the two branches of the church. It stated: "That said Methodist Episcopal Church South, of Fredericksburg, Virginia, as a church, was loyal to the Government of the United States throughout the late civil war."

They also went on to recall their original petition for reimbursement that was summarily returned by the government as "disallowed." This may explain the additional monies requested:

> *That said claim was presented to the Quartermaster-General under act of July 4, 1864, and disallowed for want of jurisdiction. That said claim was referred to the*

court April 27, 1904 by resolution of the United States Senate under act of Congress approved March 3, 1887, known as the Tucker Act. Wherefore, your petitioner prays that when the facts shall have been ascertained the same may be reported to the Senate of the United States as provided in said act of March 3, 1887.

Following the testimonies of several citizens, including church members and non-members, the summary report stated:

At the commencement of the civil war there were two Methodist Episcopal Churches in Fredericksburg, one North and one South. The building of the M.E. Church (North) is the building which was occupied by the U.S. forces and for which this claim was made. The M.E. Church (South) building was very slightly damaged from a shell and no claim was ever made on account of said building. At the close of the war the two congregations united under the M.E. Church South, and, therefore, this claim was filed on behalf of that church. P.V.D. Conway says that the congregation now owning and worshipping in this church (M.E. Church, North) is the same by succession as those who owned and worshipped there during the war.

Most of the Fredericksburg churches, Methodist included, received due payments in 1905 for the damages incurred during Federal military occupation. By then, the entire city of Fredericksburg and the surrounding Spotsylvania region had already made quite a structural and economic recovery. Thanks to an abundance of water and rail transportation, as well as a strong "industrial" center (with two flour mills, one woolen mill, a clothing factory, one silk mill, two sumac mills, three excelsior mills, one mattress factory, two pickle factories, a cannery, a shoe factory and spoke factories, as well as six repair shops), the population grew too. Additionally, the city was also a bustling trading center, with over 115 retail and wholesale businesses.

Today

In 1963, Fredericksburg United Methodist Church became the first Methodist church in the entire state of Virginia to become integrated. This groundbreaking achievement seemed appropriate as, more than one hundred years earlier, the Methodists had vehemently split over the institution of slavery. Not surprisingly, the church is currently one of the largest in town, with two thousand members, offering one worship service on Saturday and three more on Sunday morning. Now, in the twenty-first century, the congregation has increased sixfold and numerous additions have been made to the original sanctuary. The addition built in 1989 was by far the largest and was completed at a cost of a little more than $1 million. Another addition, that of a Ministry Center, was completed in 2007. In 2008, a program entitled the "Stephen Ministry" began offering a series of continuing education sessions for members of the congregation. Today, it is one of the strongest Methodist churches in the Ashland District.

Conclusion

LANDMARKS AND LEGACIES

Religious services are now held regularly every Sabbath morning at 11 o'clock in the Episcopal and Baptist Churches. Rev. Magrudar, Maury, Rector officiating at the former, and Rev. G.W. Lightner at the latter edifice.

—Fredericksburg Ledger, *May 23, 1865*

How ironic it was, that a Southern city that had been so entrenched in the middle of the Confederate rebellion would inevitably heal beneath an industrial renaissance like that experienced in the North. The complete reversal, from the slave labor–driven agricultural focus to a more mechanically driven revolution, ultimately spawned a liberating commercial and financial rebirth that left the city stronger and wealthier than before.

Understandably, the tragedies and triumphs of the Civil War remained in the hearts and minds of the town's inhabitants. In some cases it even widened a gap between many of the surviving citizens. The Secessionists, who had supported or served in the Confederate cause, were left with a bitter feeling of defeat with the South's loss. The Unionist citizens, who had voiced their loyalty in a risky and unpopular arena, were given a sense of validation with the North's victory. America would struggle to come to terms with the war and its effects for decades to come.

Certainly no one appreciated the struggle for independence more than the now-freed black citizens. The newly emancipated, who had benefited the most, began to establish their own lives within the Fredericksburg community. All sides of this social experiment, whether Secessionist, Unionist or African, had to work toward coexisting in this new racially mixed society. Fredericksburg's churches were often at the forefront of reconciliation. Many of the congregations that had been "integrated" in the prewar era reopened their doors to different ethnicities, while many minorities established their own churches as part of the process of establishing independent identities.

As time passed, wounds began to heal, yet there were battles that were still yet to come. Nearly a century later, America still struggled over equality and was divided again. The efforts to end segregation in the South formed a new civil rights movement that reinvigorated the public in the fight to establish equal rights for blacks and women. Once again, Fredericksburg weathered the storm and emerged as a stronger community.

Conclusion

Fredericksburg Bombardment, by Frank Leslie. *Courtesy Mrs. Frank Leslie, New York, 1896.*

Today, the city is a popular tourist attraction, as well as the home of the prestigious University of Mary Washington. It is also now a unique place that memorializes Confederate, Union and African American pride. The National Park Service labors year-round to present the stories of soldiers and civilians who witnessed America's "Great Divide." Monuments, museums and roadside markers bear witness to the courage and sacrifice of all who participated in the War Between the States and the descendants of the wartime townsfolk exemplify the unification that took place politically, socially and spiritually generations after the war. From the Confederate cemeteries that are maintained by the Sons of Confederate Veterans and United Daughters of the Confederacy, to the

proposed site of the National Slavery Museum, the region's memories from all sides are being preserved for future generations.

History remains Fredericksburg's most valuable commodity and its churches are an important part of the city's precious heritage. Their steadfast faith demonstrated an enduring legacy of mercy over mayhem and compassion over conflict. Each one stands today as a testament to the human spirit, teaching us through their triumphant stories about the worst and, more importantly, the best of humankind.

LOCATIONS

For those interested in visiting one of these "Houses of the Holy" in person or online:

Fredericksburg Baptist Church
1019 Princess Anne Street
Fredericksburg, VA 22401
(540) 373-4402
www.fredericksburgbaptistchurch.org

Shiloh Baptist Church (Old Site)
801 Sophia Street
Fredericksburg, VA 22401
(540) 373-8701
www.shiloholdsite.org

St. George's Episcopal Church
905 Princess Anne Street
Fredericksburg, VA 22401
(540) 373-4133
www.stgeorgesepiscopal.net

Fredericksburg Presbyterian Church
810 Princess Anne Street
Fredericksburg, VA 22401
(540) 373-7057
www.fredericksburgpc.org

Fredericksburg United Methodist Church
308 Hanover Street
Fredericksburg, VA 22401
(540) 373-9021
www.fumcva.org

Fredericksburg/Spotsylvania National Military Park
www.nps.gov/frsp

BIBLIOGRAPHY

Abbot, J.J. Letter sent with Bible from Rev. Abbot to George H. Stuart on December 22, 1864. U.S. Christian Commission. Fredericksburg/Spotsylvania National Military Park Curatorial Collection: FRSP 987, ACC 198.

Alsop, Lizzie Maxwell. Journal of Lizzie Maxwell Alsop, Fredericksburg, VA: Excerpts from July 10, September 1, September 15, September 25, 1865. Fredericksburg/Spotsylvania National Military Park, Bound Volumes #102.

Alvery, Edward, Jr. *History of the Presbyterian Church of Fredericksburg, Virginia 1808–1976.* Fredericksburg, VA: published by the Session of the Presbyterian Church Fredericksburg, Virginia, 1976.

Anderson, Frederick Jarrard. *Out of Our Hearts: The Story of Fredericksburg Baptist Church: A People On Mission.* Fredericksburg, VA: Fredericksburg Baptist Church, 2005.

Bailey, John B. Personal Diary entries December 3, 1862–December 16, 1862. Ninth New Hampshire Band.

Barbuto, Kate. "The Effects of the First Union Occupation on the Local Citizens of Fredericksburg, Virginia." Final Senior Thesis, Mary Washington College, November 2003.

Bates, Edward. Letter sent from Edward Bates to George H. Stuart on February 2, 1864. U.S. Christian Commission. Fredericksburg/Spotsylvania National Military Park Curatorial Collection: FRSP 261, ACC 23.

Broaddus, William F. Letters to Thomas B. Barton from Old Capitol Prison, August 23, 1862. Transcribed by Donald Pfanz, January 2003. Lewis Leigh Collection, U.S. Army Military History Institute, Carlisle Barracks, PA.

BIBLIOGRAPHY

Camp Life at Fredericksburg. *Durell's Battery: Excerpts on Presbyterian Church. July, 1862.* Fredericksburg/Spotsylvania National Military Park, Bound Volumes.

Catton, Bruce. *Never Call Retreat: The Centennial History of the Civil War, Volume Three.* New York: Doubleday & Company, Inc., 1965.

Child, William. *A History of the Fifth Regiment New Hampshire Volunteers.* Bristol, NH, 1893.

Claims to the U.S. Government in RG 123. Records of the U.S. Court of Claims, Entry 22, National Archives.

Coker, Francis Marion. Letter to wife from camp, 5 mi. west of Fredericksburg on December 18th, 1862. Athens, University of Georgia, Hodgson Heidler Collection.

Conway, D.M. "Fredericksburg First and Last, Section II." *Magazine of American History* 17, no. 6 (June 1887).

Court of Claims Congressional Case No. 11,616. *Trustees, Methodist Episcopal Church South of Fredericksburg, Va., v. The United States.* Entire report including petitions, letters and examination transcripts. U.S. Treasury Department, Fredericksburg/Spotsylvania National Military Park, Bound Volumes.

Court of Claims Congressional Case No. 11,781. *Trustees, Shiloh (old site) Baptist Church, Fredericksburg, Va., v. The United States.* Entire report including petitions, letters and examination transcripts. U.S. Treasury Department, Fredericksburg/Spotsylvania National Military Park, Bound Volumes.

Court of Claims Congressional Case No. 11,786. *Baptist Church of Fredericksburg, Virginia v. The United States.* Entire report including petitions, letters and examination transcripts. U.S. Treasury Department, Fredericksburg/Spotsylvania National Military Park, Bound Volumes.

Court of Claims Congressional Case No. 11,793. *Presbyterian Church of Fredericksburg, Va., v. The United States.* Entire report including petitions, letters and examination transcripts. U.S. Treasury Department, Fredericksburg/Spotsylvania National Military Park, Bound Volumes.

Davies, Reverend Lawrence A. "Fredericksburg National Cemetery for African Americans, a Tangible Reminder of Liberty." Speech, Memorial Day, 2006.

Felder, Paula S. *Forgotten Companions: The First Settlers of Spotsylvania County and Fredericksburgh Town (With Notes on Early Land Use).* Fredericksburg/Spotsylvania National Military Park, Bound Volumes.

Fredericksburg and the Cavalier County. *Cannon Balls: Excerpts on Presbyterian Church.* Fredericksburg/Spotsylvania National Military Park, Bound Volumes.

Fredericksburg Baptist Church. "The Church on a Hill: Commemorative Brochure." Contributions by Mildred Powell, church historian.

Fredericksburg Ledger. "Article on Religious Services returning at Baptist and Episcopal Churches," May 23, 1865.

Gerrish. *Reminiscences of the War: My Second Visit 20th Maine, 3rd Brigade, 5th Corps.*

Goolrick, William K., and the editors of Time-Life Books. *The Civil War: Rebels Resurgent: Fredericksburg to Chancellorsville.* New York: Time-Life Books, 1985.

Gramling, Wilber Wightman. Excerpts from the Diary of Wilber Wightman Gramling: May 6, 1864–May 5, 1865. Fredericksburg/Spotsylvania National Military Park, Bound Volumes #244.

Harrison, Noel G. *Fredericksburg Civil War Sites: April 1861–November 1862, 1st Edition.* Appomattox, VA: H.E. Howard Inc., 1995.

———. *Fredericksburg Civil War Sites: December 1862–April 1865, Volume Two.* Appomattox, VA: H.E. Howard Inc., 1995.

Hennessy, John. *Notes on St. George's Episcopal Church & The Baptist Church During the Civil War: A Documentary Record.* Fredericksburg/Spotsylvania National Military Park.

Historic Fredericksburg Foundation Inc. "Research prepared for Shiloh Baptist Church (Old Site): A Brief History of the Church." Principal researcher, Laura Farwell, March 2000.

History of Forsyth County, Georgia. Letter from Josiah B. Patterson to wife from Fredericksburg, VA on March 28, 1862. Easley, SC: Southern History Press, 1985.

Hoopes, John W. (Christopher (Kit) Mott Camp 1379). *The Confederate Memoir of William M. Abernathy.* Confederate Veteran, Volume Two, 2003 SCV Publications.

Jaynes, Gregory, and the editors of Time-Life Books. *The Civil War: The Killing Ground: Wilderness to Cold Harbor.* New York: Time-Life Books, 1985.

Jefferson County News. "Account of 35th New York and The Retreat of Gen. Banes," May 29, 1862.

BIBLIOGRAPHY

Johnson, John Janney. *John Kobler's Dream: A History of the Fredericksburg United Methodist Church 1802–1975.* Fredericksburg, VA: J. Johnson, 1976.

Jones, J. William. *Christ In The Camp.* Richmond, VA: B.F. Johnson & Co., 1887; Martin & Hoyt Co., 1904; Penn Laird, VA: Sprinkle Publications, 1986.

Jones, J. William, with an introduction by Reverend J.C. Granberry, DD. *Religion In Lee's Army.* Richmond, VA: B.F. Johnson & Co., 1888.

Justice, Benjamin W. Justice (second lieutenant, Forty-seventh North Carolina). Letter to wife from near Orange Court House, Virginia, November 22, 1863.

Little Rock Weekly Arkansas Gazette. "For the State Gazette. A Tale of the Revolution. An Ower [*sic*] True Tale," September 13, 1862.

London Times. "Eyewitness account of damage to the city of Fredericksburg," January 23, 1863.

Lovell, Dr. Harry. Letters to Ellen, Fredericksburg, VA March 1863. Provided by Gary M. Elmund, transcribed by Robert K. Krick, Fredericksburg/Spotsylvania National Military Park.

Miscellaneous Church Session Minutes (1860–1877) provided by individual church historians: Fredericksburg Baptist Church, Shiloh Baptist (Old Site), St. George's Episcopal Church, Fredericksburg Presbyterian Church, Fredericksburg United Methodist Church (Private Collections).

Moore, John S., ed. "The Prison Diary of William F. Broaddus." Edited by W. Harrison Daniel. *The Virginia Baptist Register: Annual Publication of the Virginia Historical Society,* no. 21 (1982).

Neisingh, Liesbeth. *Fredericksburg Area Churches, Volumes 343–346.* Letters to Secretary of War E.M. Stanton from M.E. Meigs, quartermaster general U.S.A., petition to the Senate and House of Representatives of the United States of America in Congress assembled. Fredericksburg/Spotsylvania National Military Park. Assembled March 2000.

Nick, William. Letter sent to wife from Rockbridge Artillery camp, December 17, 1862. Accompanied by an article titled "A Letter Yellow with Age Tells of Fredericksburg Fight." Fredericksburg/Spotsylvania National Military Park Curatorial Collection: FRSP 2326, ACC 252.

Philadelphia Weekly Times. "Annals of the War: Battle of Fredericksburg by Major General St. Clair A. Mulholland," Saturday April 23, 1881.

Pierce, Major F.E. Misc. Letters, Headquarters 108 Regiment, N.Y.S. Vol's. Near Fredericksburg, December 17, 1862. Washington, D.C.: United States Department of the Interior, National Park Service, 1933.

Quenzel, Carrol H. *The History and Background of St. George's Episcopal Church Fredericksburg, Virginia.* Fredericksburg, VA: Vestry of St. George's Episcopal Church, 1951.

Quenzel, Carrol H., with Mr. George H.S. King. Burials in St. George's Graveyard: From "The History of St. George's Episcopal Church." Brochure, 1951.

Randolph, Reverend Alfred Magill. "Series of letters to wife, Fredericksburg, February– May 1863. Randolph Family Papers Mss1R1586b, Virginia Historical Society, Richmond, VA.

Rochester Daily Union & Advertiser. "Misc. article clippings: From the 140th Regiment in Camp Near Fredericksburg, VA," December 18, 1862.

Sanford, Colonel George B. *Fighting Rebels and Redskins: Experiences in Army Life of Colonel George B. Sanford 1861–1892.* Edited by E.R. Hagemann. Norman: University of Oklahoma Press, 1969.

Schlesinger, Nelda, ed. *Frederick Joseph Wilt, His Life and Civil War Letters.* New Athens, IL, 1992.

Shibley, Robert. *In Fredericksburg: The Past & Presence of an Old Virginia Town.* Photographs by Taylor Lewis. New York: Parson Weems Press, 1984.

Shiloh Baptist Church (Old Site). 1855–1856 Church Minutes & Membership Rolls w/ May, 1856 Colored Congregation dismissals. Shiloh Baptist Archives, Private Collection.

———. "Fiftieth Anniversary and Jubilee: Jubilee Jottings." Commemorative program, 1914.

———. *History of Shiloh Baptist Church (Old Site), Historical Time Line, Early History (through 1878), Members of our church in the 1854–1856 time period.* 2007.

Smith, James Power. Notes of Rev. James Power Smith, D.D. Fredericksburg/Spotsylvania National Military Park, Bound Volumes #091.

Southern Confederacy. "Scene and Incidents Connected with the Battle of Fredericksburg." Atlanta Georgia News, December 27, 1862.

Star newspaper. "Colored Churches," July 26, 1890.

St. George's Episcopal Church. *A Brief History of St. George's Church: A Historical Overview, Chronology of Highlights, Seating Plan of St. George's Church in 1849.*

―――. Miscellaneous letters, newspaper clippings and minutes: Return of stolen Communion Set. Subsequent church minutes from June 1931. Private collection.

Stiles, Robert. *Four Years Under Marse Robert*. Introduction and index by Robert K. Krick. Dayton, OH: Morningside Bookshop, 1977.

Sturges, Mrs. Jonathan. *Reminiscences Of A Long Life*. New York: F.R. Parrish and Company, 1894.

Todd Reminiscences. *#722: On Post In The Church Steeple*. Southern Historical Society Collection, University of North Carolina Library, Chapel Hill.

United States Army Official Hospital Index, 2nd Army Corps. *Locations of Second Corps Field Hospitals in Fredericksburg Virginia, May 9–25, 1864*. Transcribed by Donald Pfanz, August 2001. National Archives, Washington, D.C.

United States Senate. Declaration of Resolve: Announcing all claims of trustees of the Fredericksburg Churches approved under the Tucker Act. Note: This document contains all Court of Claims Case Nos. February 28, 1905.

Walker, Joseph F. *Life of Joseph F. Walker Fredericksburg, VA*. Postwar slave narrative, transcribed by John J. Lanier. Collection of Fredericksburg Area Museum and Cultural Center.

Washington, John. *Memories of the Past*. Postwar slave narrative. Library of Congress. Acc. No. 16,842. transcribed by the National Park Service 1984. Prewar material transcribed by Fitzgerald and Willis.

Wheelock, Julia S. *The Boys in White; the Experiences of a Hospital Agent in and Around Washington*. New York, 1870.

Wood, Thomas Fanning. *Doctor To The Front: The Civil War Journal of Thomas Fanning Wood, M.D. 1861–1865*. Edited by Donald B. Koonce. Knoxville: University of Tennessee Press, Spectrum Communications, 1997.

Internet Sources

Fredericksburg Baptist Church, www.fredericksburgbaptistchurch.org.

Fredericksburg Presbyterian Church, www.fredericksburgpc.org.

Fredericksburg/Spotsylvania National Military Park, www.nps.gov/frsp.

Fredericksburg United Methodist Church, www.fumcva.org.

Shiloh Baptist Church (Old Site), www.shiloholdsite.org.

St. George's Episcopal Church, www.stgeorgesepiscopal.net.

ABOUT THE AUTHOR

Historian Michael Aubrecht has dedicated his studies to the role of Christianity during the Civil War. He is the author of numerous articles and books on the subject, including *Onward Christian Soldier*, *Christian Cavalier* and *The Southern Cross*. From 2000 to 2006, Michael authored over 375 separate studies on the history of America's national pastime for *Baseball-Almanac*, as well as the eBook *Luckiest Fans On The Face Of This Earth: The History of New York Yankees Fall Classics*. In 2004, Michael joined the online authors group Faith Writers and began writing Christian material that has been published in multiple religious magazines and periodicals. He has also been active as a contributing writer for the *Spotsylvania Presbyterian Church Post*. Today, Michael writes historical features and book reviews for the *Free Lance-Star* newspaper and *Civil War Historian* magazine. Michael is also a founding member of the Jackson Society, an associate member of the Sons of Confederate Veterans (Camp #1296), an honorary member of the John Bell Hood Historical Society, a proud supporter of the Gettysburg Foundation and an experienced speaker. He currently resides in historic Fredericksburg, Virginia, with his wife and four children. For more information, visit Michael's website and blog at www.pinstripepress.net.